First Victory of the World Proletariat

The Paris Commune

**INTERNATIONAL
COMMUNIST PARTY**

www.international-communist-party.org

First published as "La Commune de Paris, 1871, Première victoire du prolétariat mondial" in *La Gauche Communiste*, Numbers 9–10, January–December 1985
Translation, layout and cover by the ICP

UK: ICP Editions c/o 96 Bold Street, Liverpool L1 4HY

US: CL Publishing c/o PO Box 14344, Portland, OR 97293

Italy: Associazione la Sinistra Comunista, Casella Postale 1157, 50121 Firenze

ISBN: 9781312607422

THE INTERNATIONAL COMMUNIST PARTY

WHAT DISTINGUISHES OUR PARTY—The line running from Marx to Lenin to the foundation of the Third International and the birth of the Communist Party of Italy in Leghorn (Livorno) 1921, and from there to the struggle of the Italian Communist Left against the degeneration in Moscow and to the rejection of popular fronts and coalitions of resistance groups – The tough work of restoring the revolutionary doctrine and the party organ, in contact with the working class, outside the realm of personal politics and electoralist manoevrings.

www.international-communist-party.org
Communications to
icparty@interncommparty.org

Contents

Presentation

To resume the history of the French workers' movement

This study on the Paris Commune is part of a wider work on the workers' movement in France undertaken by our Party, following what had been done in the sixties. Reclaiming our own history, that of our class, is a vital necessity for the objectives we set ourselves, the communist revolution and the establishment of the dictatorship of the proletariat, the logical outcome of the long tormented journey of humanity. The restoration of the doctrine goes through the study of the proletarian movement, of its defeats as well as its victories, in order to draw all possible lessons from it that will be profitable for the resumption of the class movement on these healthy bases. This work is done in conjunction with the vast research on the History of the Communist Left in these crucial 1920s, work and continuity that we are, here again, alone in pursuing serenely.

We wanted to describe the main events from July 1870 to May 1871, the forces in presence, the errors committed, the objective inadequacies, the lessons to be drawn from them, taking care not to fall into the tearful cult of the memory of the martyrs which has only one goal: to erase any useful lesson for the future resumption of the proletarian movement.

The text consists of two parts, which we briefly summarize here.

The labor movement in the 1860s was experiencing a renaissance, both politically and in terms of trade unions, so that a revolutionary situation was reached as early as 1858. This precipitated the government of Napoleon III, not supported by the bourgeoisie, into the war against Prussia—with the immediate aim of preventing the reunification of that country.

The first part, from war to revolution (from July 1870 to 18 March 1871), explains the military disaster of the Second Empire, a regime which collapsed... without the proletariat knowing how to seize the opportunity to take power. However, it imposed the Republic on the bourgeoisie on 4 September, and organized itself into neighborhood committees and a Central Committee.

On 30 September, the proletariat again missed a great opportunity; the capitulation on 2 January 1871 discredited even more the bourgeoisie who asks Bismarck to occupy Paris. It refuses.

Elected by the "rural" people, the National Assembly and Thiers at its head hastily concluded a peace that was very expensively paid to Bismarck, and then took various measures against Paris.

The night of 17–18 March is marked by the abortive attempt to retake the guns of the National Guard: the troops fraternize with the proletariat. Thiers, panic-stricken, flees to Versailles.

The second part deals strictly speaking with the Paris Commune, from 18 March to 28 May 1871.

A true universal republic, the Commune behaves as the only legal government in France: we can speak of the first dictatorship of the proletariat. With 10,000 employees (instead of 60,000 before), the Commune administers Paris: it is a real "cheap government". Within it, all the organizations of the proletariat come back to life.

Unfortunately, the proletariat hardly has the initiative. It's the bourgeoisie which quickly returns to the offensive, stirring up the civil war which the communards don't dare to take up, staying in defensive positions. The only exit in the direction of Versailles is a disaster.

In May, the balance of power shifted in favor of Versailles, thanks to the prisoners freed by Bismarck. On the 21st, the Versailles people entered Paris, because of treason, and Thiers gave the order for a general massacre. Although the communards fought heroically, they were once again the victims of the lack of a military strategy, or rather the worst possible one proclaimed by Delescluze: fighting quarter by quarter.

From 21 to 28 May, the bloody week: 30,000 Parisians killed, 45,000 arrested, many of whom were shot. In total, summing up deaths and deportations, Paris loses 100,000 of its sons, many of them women and children.

The text then reviews the attitude of Marx and Engels, and of the International Working Men's Association (IWMA) to French events, and draws the two cardinal lessons of the Paris Commune. The Commune marked the end of utopian socialism, the beginning of the era of scientific socialism; it sanctioned the defeat of Marxism in France: it took Guesde and Lafargue a good ten years to learn the lessons of the Commune and found the French Workers' Party in 1882, the first independent French proletarian party.

The first lesson: if 1848 had shown the necessity of political power, the Commune demonstrates something else: this power, this bourgeois State, cannot be used. "The destruction of the bourgeois State, an essential deduction in the Marxist doctrine of the State" (Lenin), through the establishment of the dictatorship of the proletariat, is one of the central points of the communist program that we claim 100%. Not because we want to be distinguished "purists", but because Marxism is a construction that must be accepted or rejected as a whole: one cannot accept the "originality" of historical materialism and put aside the

Marxist theory of the State or of violence without brazenly betraying communism.

The ex-Institut Maurice Thorez (the creative elite of French national communists), "celebrated" in its own way the centenary of the Commune, by organizing a colloquium on 6–7–8 May 1971 in Paris. On the question of the State, only one "contribution", that of...Guy Mollet, the old social-democratic bastard who has on his hands the blood of the miners of the North (he created the Compagnies Républicaines de Sécurité to intervene against them in 1947) and of thousands of proletarians of ex-Indochina and Algeria (his government voted, all parties taken together, the credits to the military in 1954). Our Stalinists, in the depths of their doctrinal nullity, have listened to the insanities (which they defend first!)...spouted by a "much-hated socialist". It is true that in the denial and falsification of communist principles, these carrions are worth their weight in gold.

The second lesson: 1871 marks a change of historical era, at least for the European area. There are no more progressive bourgeois wars, but only imperialist wars, to which the proletariat must not give its support. 1871 ends the era, for all of Western Europe, of double revolutions and progressive national wars.

> 1871 is a clear turning-point in history. The struggle against Napoleon III and his dictatorship is in fact directed against a capitalistic and not a feudal form; it is at the same time the product and proof of the mobilisation of the two fundamental and enemy classes of modern society. Although it sees in Napoleon an obstacle to the bourgeois development of Germany, revolutionary Marxism goes immediately on the side of the anti-bourgeois struggle which will be that of all parties of the Commune, first workers' dictatorship in history....The response to the second wave [of opportunism]was another tactical formula: no war alliances (since 1871) with the State and bourgeoisie. (*Characteristic Theses of the Party*, 1951)

From 1871, with the crushing of the Commune, "all the European bourgeois armies are allied against the proletariat" (Marx). The continental countries of Western Europe then joined the situation of England: the bourgeois revolution is accomplished, national unity has been achieved everywhere, only proletarian revolution is on the agenda.

So many lies about the work of the Commune!

Also for the centenary, opportunism, skillful and trained in destructive commemorations, had put huge panels against the Mur des Fédérés, with the inscription: "The struggle for democracy and socialism is the Commune still alive"...

This is indeed the fundamental trait of opportunism: to laminate the proletarian movement by concealing or deforming its strong points. Destroy Marxism by "enriching" it! Let's oppose this simple passage from our *Dialogue with the Dead* (1957): "We already know a lot about this "enrichment": democratic passage of power to the "communists"; imperialism without war; renunciation of the use of violence; constitutional discipline; imitation of capitalism considered as a factory of welfare; honest competition with it; signed promise not to trick it, made today in London, tomorrow in Washington. Enrich Marxism just a little bit more in this way...and you will have torn it to pieces!"

Yes, the Commune is quite the opposite of that!

It lays down in black and white the vital importance of the military question, the hatred of the bourgeoisie, which is consequential—it is capable of the worst massacres to see its power maintained, like any ruling class—the crucial question of the centralised and independent party, a real general staff without which no victory is possible in the face of a hyper-centralized and armed class and State, a party and party dictatorship that have been cruelly lacking.

For the bourgeoisie, all means are good. Let's listen to the "Officiel de Versailles" giving its orders: "Since, as of 18th March, the army had not raised its rifle butts in the air, the soldiers were stuffed with alcohol mixed, according to the old recipe, with gunpowder..." (in Louise Michel, *La Commune*, Stock 1978, p.303).

The same process was used during the First World War in France, and is commonly used throughout the world today.

How far could the class hatred of the bourgeoisie go? "But as everywhere was full of dead people, the smell of the huge grave drew the horrible swarm of meat flies from the mass graves to the dead city, and the victors, fearing the plague, suspended executions (op.cit. p.326)." Modern methods remove these sanitary barriers, which are the only (and only!) obstacle to the threatened bourgeoisie's remedy.

Our 1951 text *Proletarian Dictatorship and Class Party* reformulates the question of the State and explains the central role of the party, a role which will not diminish but take on ever more crucial importance as the productive forces and class antagonisms develop.

The party is necessary BEFORE the proletarian revolution: its task is the elaboration and diffusion of communist theory. It assures the continuity of the proletarian organization and prepares the offensive for the conquest of power.

The party is necessary DURING the proletarian revolution: it consciously leads it in order to ensure its victory; the choice is simply and unambiguously summed up: either destroy the bourgeois State or crush the revolution.

The party is necessary AFTER the proletarian revolution, in the phase of building socialism, in the defense of the new proletarian State erected on the ruins of the old one against any sign of revenge on the part of the now dominated classes, by all means. This proletarian State will be an open class dictatorship led by the Communist Party, and, like the Paris Commune, will sweep away the legislative-executive distinction which is characteristic of bourgeois regimes. The progressive abolition of classes will lead to the disappearance of the organ of domination by the working class, the proletarian State.

To the dictatorship of the bourgeoisie MUST respond the dictatorship of the proletariat; to bourgeois violence MUST respond proletarian violence, organized and aiming at the greatest efficiency in the interest of the proletariat, of communism.

The party is present everywhere in this tormented process: on the theoretical, trade union, political, military level...; it is not bound to any code, except that of class warfare: may the strongest and best prepared win, and woe to the defeated!

Democracy and Liberty: these are the two poisons that opportunism breathed into the working class yesterday, the same poisons that it distills day and night to the proletariat today. It is against these "lying cries" that the text of the Archives rises, constituting the guiding thread of the work on the Commune, which we recommend to our readers.

Part I
FROM WAR TO REVOLUTION

1. DYNASTIC WARFARE

From the declaration of war on 19 July 1870 to the capitulation of 23 January 1871

a. Circumstances and causes

The clash of Gallic and Teutonic imperialism with the rise of social struggles

Napoleonic imperialism had long been eyeing the German left bank of the Rhine and flattered the chauvinism of a large part of the French population. The Austro-Prussian War of 1866 aroused the appetite of the little Bonapartist cockerel; in exchange for his neutrality in the conflict, Bismarck had promised Napoleon III territorial compensation, which he never actually received. In his 1891 introduction to *The Civil War in France*, Engels writes:

> But the Second Empire was a call for French chauvinism, a demand for the borders of the First Empire, lost in 1814, or at least those of the First Republic...But there was no conquest that fascinated the imagination of French chauvinists as much as that of the German left bank of the Rhine (...) Once the Second Empire was a fact, the claim to the left bank of the Rhine, either all at once or piecemeal, was only a matter of time. The time came with the Austro-Prussian War of 1866; cheated of the anticipated "territorial compensation" by Bismarck, and by his own over-cunning, hesitating policy, there was now nothing left for Napoleon but war, which broke out in 1870 and drove him first to Sedan, and then to Wilhelmshöhe. (M-E, XXVII, 182)

The war of 1870 was thus already looming in 1866, as Engels points out ("The role of violence in history. The role of violence and the economy in the establishment of the new German empire", in *Military Writings*, (M-E, XXVI, 484): "Bismarck not only knew that the peace with Austria was pregnant with war with France, he also desired it. This war was to provide the means of perfecting the Prusso-German Empire demanded of him by the German bourgeoisie."

Napoleon III and Bismarck both wanted war.

The first one to restore its coat of arms, solve its internal problems and break the proletarian threat which was at its height because of the economic crisis. The second to seal German national unity under the aegis of Prussia, through a war common to the States of the South and the North, and thus to achieve unity from above by dispensing with the proletarian and bourgeois classes, contrary to the French model. Germany was then only a federation of independent States divided into northern and southern States (Bavaria, Württemberg, Grand Duchy of Baden, etc.). There were 16 northern States, which had been united since 1866 in a confederation presided over by the King of Prussia. The two northern States, Prussia and Hesse, the richest of the German States, were also experiencing an industrial crisis with social unrest.

After 1866 the relations between the two countries had become increasingly tense. The pretext was to be provided by the question of the succession to the Spanish throne for which Prussia had proposed the candidature of the Prince of Hohenzollern. France violently opposed this because of the risk of a Berlin-Madrid axis being created, and demanded the withdrawal of this provocative candidacy. King William of Prussia, who was on holiday in the spa town of Elms, sent a telegram on 13 July officially confirming to France that he had withdrawn his candidacy. Bismarck intercepted this *dispatch from Elms*", Bismark disguised a king's dispatch in such a way as to suggest that the King of Prussia had dismissed the French ambassador, and published it in the Cologne Gazette. This manoeuvre "produced on the Gallic bull the effect of a red rag", and led the French government to declare war on Prussia on 19 July 1870.

Who then allowed Louis Bonaparte to wage war on Germany? And Marx replied: PRUSSIA! (M-E, XXII, 5-6):

> Let us not forget that it was the rulers and the ruling classes of Europe who allowed Louis Bonaparte to play the ferocious farce of the *restored Empire* for eighteen years...It was Bismarck who conspired with this same Louis Bonaparte, in order to crush the popular opposition inside and to annex Germany to the Hohenzollern dynasty...The Bonapartist regime, which until then had flourished only on one bank of the Rhine, now had its counterpart on the other bank...with its effective despo-

tism and cardboard democratism, its political *trompe l'oeil* and financial fiddling, its snoring phraseology and its vile tricks.

Bismarck leads the game

The Prussian army was morally and technically prepared. Since 1857 it was led by an excellent soldier, Helmut Von Moltke, who turned the army into a modern corps. He had experience of European battles with the victorious war against Austria in 1866 and had already developed plans for the methodical preparation of the war against France with plans for mobilising and transporting troops. It had 462,000 men, 57,000 horsemen, 80,000 horses. Six railway lines were laid out between the Rhine and the Moselle for the transport of troops. It thus had two major assets: a rapid movement of troops, and fire power with heavy artillery and cannons that carried further than the French.

Indeed France was not ready!! The French officers had no experience of European warfare and moreover suffered from self-sufficiency. Nothing was seriously prepared. The French troops left for Germany without maps of Alsace and Lorraine, which made them get lost many times! The French railways were developed but not organized militarily. The army had fewer soldiers than the Prussian army (to which were to be added those of the other States), a larger but useless cavalry, mediocre heavy artillery; only the chassepot rifle was technically superior to that of the enemy!

As Engels wrote in 1887 (M-E, XXVI, 487-488), Louis Napoleon was taken by surprise:

> He not only saw that he had walked into a trap, he also knew that his emperorship was at stake, and he had little confidence in the faithfulness of his Bonapartist Brimstone gang, who assured him that everything was ready, up to the last button on the men's spats, and even less confidence in their military and administrative skill. But the logical consequences of his own past drove him towards destruction; his hesitation itself hastened his doom. Bismarck, on the other hand, was not only quite ready for action militarily, but this time he actually had the people behind him, who saw only one fact behind the diplomatic lies spread by both sides: namely, that this was a war not only for the Rhine, but for national existence…All class differences vanished in the face of this national upsurge.

The French bourgeoisie was also very surprised by the announcement of the war, for which it initially had an attitude of refusal. Still in the first Address, Marx explains: "The war plot of July, 1870, is but an amended edition of the coup d'état of December, 1851. At first view the thing seemed so absurd that France would not believe in its real good earnest…When, on July 15th, war was at last officially announced to the *Corps Législatif*, the whole opposition refused to vote the preliminary subsidies, even Thiers branded it as 'detestable'; all the independent journals of Paris condemned it, and, wonderful to relate, the provincial press joined in almost unanimously" (M-E, XXII, 4). The war credits were eventually voted.

Marshal Bazaine was appointed on 12 August in the middle of the war as commander-in-chief of the Rhine army, which represented all the French armed forces; he had served in Algeria, the Crimea and Mexico. Marshal Patrice de Mac Mahon, a convinced monarchist, was given command of the first corps of the Rhine army in Alsace on 17 July.

A war of defense on the German side

The conflict thus takes on the aspect of a war in defense of Germany against French aggression; it expresses French imperialism's desire to prevent German unity and to annex the left bank of the Rhine. Emperor Wilhelm I will hypocritically state in his speech from the throne that this is a war against Napoleon III, not a war against the French people, a defensive war, not an offensive war. And the German States answered the call of the German "fatherland". Bismarck had won!

b. Attitude of labor movements

As early as 1866, the threat of war loomed over Europe. In July 1866, the Paris office of the International Workingmen's Association (IWMA) advised neutrality to the workers. An appeal was launched by the workers of Berlin in favor of peace, to which the Paris office of the IWMA, with Varlin, Tolain and Freiburg, responded with a manifesto calling for the abolition of standing armies and the organization of national militias.

Then comes the scandal of the affair of the republican journalist Victor Noir. Prince Pierre Bonaparte, the emperor's cousin, killed the journalist who had come to organize a duel between the prince and the editor-in-chief of the anti-Bonapartist newspaper La Marseillaise on 10 January 1870. 100,000 people attend his funeral in Neuilly sur Seine on 12 January. Among the crowd were Eugène Varlin, Louise Michel, Jean Baptiste Millière. An anti-Napoleonic agitation begins. Charles Delescluze, chief editor of the republican newspaper Le réveil and supporters of the International call for calm. Pierre Bonaparte will be acquitted in March.

On 12 July 1870, the Parisian members of the IWMA published another manifesto "to the workers of all countries", followed by many addresses of other organizations fully supporting the Paris office's protest against the war. Threats of war also gave rise to workers' demonstrations, as Marx points out in the first address of 23 July 1870, in *The Civil War in France*: "…the real workmen of the Faubourgs came forward with public peace demonstrations so overwhelming that Piétri, the Prefect of Police, thought it prudent to at once stop all further street politics…" (M-E, XXII, 5).

Marx, in the same text, recalls the reactions of the German workers. They responded to the call for peace from the French workers. In principle, the German working class opposed the war because Bismarck wanted to consolidate Prussia's predominance in Germany and to make German unity not from below with popular support, but from above; in practice, it did not have the strength to oppose it and it accepted the war as a necessary and inevitable evil. "With deep regret and pain we are forced to submit to a war of defense as an inevitable evil." This was expressed by a mass workers' meeting held in Brunswick on July 16, 1870. In Chemnitz, a meeting of delegates representing 50,000 Saxon workers unanimously adopted the following resolution: "We declare that the present war is exclusively dynastic…We are happy to grasp the fraternal hand that the workers of France are extending to us."

But in France, the war which was going to mobilize the workers, increase misery and unemployment, was also going to lead to the collapse of the workers' organizations which had developed extraordinarily in the preceding years, that is to say the IWMA and the workers' societies. The declaration of war of July 1870 by the Bonapartist government would be the first blow to this vigorously growing workers' movement; the second blow that the international bourgeoisie would want to be fatal would be, with the Paris Commune and other cities of France, to savagely and definitively crush—or so it believed—its mortal enemy.

c. The French military debacle

Bazaine's retreat in Metz on 16th August and Napoleon III's surrender in Sedan on 2nd September

...the death knell of the Second Empire has already sounded at Paris. It will end as it began, by a parody." (M-E, XXII, 5). This was Marx's sentence in the First Address of 23-7-1870. French society, after 18 years of the "Lower Empire" (as Engels said), was undermined by corruption, the negligence of the Bonapartist system; it could not face the conflict honorably and the Empire collapsed like a "house of cards" (Engels, Introduction to *The Civil War...*, 1891).

From July 1870 to February 1871, Engels followed the events very closely and produced about sixty military articles on the Franco-Prussian War. In 1887 he wrote:

> Louis Napoleon's army was defeated in every battle and finally three-quarters of it went to Germany as prisoners of war. This was not the fault of the soldiers, who had fought bravely enough, but of the leaders and the administration. But if, like Louis Napoleon, one had created an empire with the help of a gang of rascals, if this empire had been maintained for eighteen years merely by abandoning France to the exploitation of that gang, if all decisive posts in the state had been filled with people belonging to that very gang and all subordinate posts with their accomplices, then one should not engage in a life-and-death battle if one does not wish to be left in the lurch. The entire edifice of the empire that had been the admiration of European philistines for years crashed in less than five weeks; the revolution of September 4 simply cleared away the rubble, and Bismarck, who had gone to war to found a small German empire, turned out one fine morning to be the founder of a French republic (M-E, XXVI, 488-489).

And Marx wrote to Engels on August 8, 1870: "Quite in accordance with the spirit of the LOWER EMPIRE, we can see how in this war—in its commissariat and its diplomacy—everyone acts in obedience to the maxim: steal from one another and lie to one another" (M.E, XLIV, 39-40).

Thus, on 4 August, the troops of the Empire suffered their first defeats. The imperial army, launched into an offensive strategy (invading enemy territory through the country of Baden and cutting northern Germany off from southern Germany) was forced to go on the defensive because the Prussians had gained speed by invading the two border regions themselves: Alsace defended by General Mac Mahon, and Lorraine defended by Generals Frossart and Bazaine.

On August 3, 1870, Engels wrote to Marx: "If the noble Louis had attacked on Friday he could have got as far as the Rhine without much trouble. But by Tuesday the Germans must be more or less ready. His best chance of taking the offensive was frustrated through his own fault—i.e. by the bas empire, by the JOBBERY in the army administration which delayed him for 5 days and has probably forced him to march in before he was ready" (M-E, XLIV, 13). And on 5 August 1870: "We have never seen such a waste."

The Marshal of France Patrice de Mac Mahon, Count of Mac Mahon, a convinced monarchist, who had commanded the first corps of the army of the Rhine since 17 July 1870, was to accumulate errors in Alsace.

Indeed, Bavarian troops with Prussian troops, 60,000 men, arrived in Northern Alsace, in Wissembourg dominated by a military citadel. This is the real starting point of the war. General Douay and his troops (8,000 men) were sent there, because of the supplies there, to organize baker's brigades to supply the army. The cavalry, which had gone on reconnaissance, did not detect the presence of enemy troops. The attack was therefore a surprise. The small town of Wissembourg is bombed. The Bavarian attacks are heroically repulsed, but after the arrival of Prussian troops, General Douay decides to retire. He will be killed by a shrapnel. The battalion commander, Liaud, decides to stay to defend the small town of Bitche with its citadel. The siege by Bavarian troops will last until the end of the war; despite the bombardment of the town and the losses, the citadel will not want to surrender.

The army of Alsace withdraws with serious losses on Chalons-sur-Marne: 2300 killed on the French side against 1551 on the German side. Marshal Mac Mahon is forced to retreat to fight around Woerth-Froeschwiller. It is there the disastrous battle of Reichshoffen of August 6th where to cover his retreat, Mac Mahon will sacrifice the Algerian riflemen numbering 1700 of which 800 were massacred by enemy machine-gun fire. This battle also remains marked by a series of deadly and useless charges by French cuirassiers against German guns.

The mistakes made on the French side would be repeated throughout the war. Whilst the Prussian leaders marched with cannon, the French stayed put. The artillery was numerically inferior and the range of the French guns was also inferior to that of the Germans. All the weight of the battle rested on the infantry, which was exemplary and brave, like the Algerian riflemen, but which could defeat an army superior in numbers and better equipped with guns. The fighting was a series of carnage, massacres and visions of horror that haunted soldiers on both sides for a long time!

The bulk of the Rhine army led by the Marshal of France Bazaine operated in Lorraine. On August 16, to the general astonishment, he decided to withdraw his army of 180,000 men to Metz, thus allowing himself to be cut off from Free France. The fortress of Metz was immediately assailed by the Prussians and thus began a siege which ended on October 27th with the capitulation of Bazaine.

On 9 August, the Ollivier ministry falls. Empress Eugenie, regent, replaces him with a dynastic defense cabinet headed by general Count Palikao. On the 23rd, Eugénie and Palikao force the army of Châlons led by Napoleon and Mac Mahon to march towards the army of Bazaine, surrounded in Metz. It is thus a series of orders and counter-orders for the soldiers who thus turn in circles. Informed by the newspapers, the Prussian chief of staff sends troops in the direction of Chalons in front of the French troops who are indecisive and wander as far as Sedan.

This sad epic ends with the disastrous fighting on 31 August and 1 September in Beaumont and around Sedan, on the road to Metz. The French troops numbered around 120,000 men and 564 cannons commanded by General Mac Mahon (wounded, he would be replaced by General Auguste Alexandre Ducrot). In the other, there were 200,000 soldiers (Prussia and Bavaria) commanded by Von Moltke with 774 cannons. King William of Prussia and Bismarck will witness the fighting from the top of a hill. The battle left 28,000 French dead and wounded, compared to 3,000 killed and 6,000 wounded Germans. Surrounded and completely disorganized, the French army retreated in disorder inside the citadel town of Sedan. It was a terrified flood of men, horses, wagons, cannons mingling, crashing, and all under the bombs. Faced with this debacle, Napoleon III gave the order to hoist the white flag to request an armistice on 1 September. Bismarck demands an unconditional surrender and refuses to allow Napoleon III to meet King William to negotiate. On September 2, Napoleon III is taken to the Château de Bellevue, which dominates the Meuse and the town of Sedan, to sign the act of surrender with the generals in chief of both sides and the two sovereigns. This act specifies that the stronghold as well as arms, munitions, equipment, horses and flags will be handed over to the victors and that the captured army will be taken to the Iges peninsula west of Sedan. 550 officers who give their word that they will no longer fight the

Germans for the duration of the war are released immediately and will thus be able to reinforce the ranks of the reactionaries. 6,000 horses and 419 cannons are delivered. The Emperor and some of his officers are held in a golden prison at Wilhemshöhe Castle in Hesse. Field Marshal Mac Mahon is detained in Wiesbaden and released in March 1871. 83,000 soldiers and officers are held in an open-air camp on the Meuse River on the Iges peninsula, without shelter or food. Many die of hunger and disease. The camp will be gradually evacuated to Germany and will remain a desolate landscape.

The 2nd September, the day of the French surrender, became a bank holiday of the German Empire until 1918.

The fall of Napoleon should have put an end to the war, since Bismarck and William I had proclaimed that the war was directed against Bonaparte and not against the French people, but it did not happen... The Prussian armies and their allies stormed northern France to lay siege to Paris.

2. THE CONSEQUENCES OF THE DEBACLE

a. The Republic was proclaimed on 4 September 1870!

The revolution of 4 September 1870: Saving the fatherland in danger

At the beginning of August, popular demonstrations against the Empire and its first military defeats had broken out in Paris. On 14 August, Blanqui and his friends had even tried to set Paris against Napoleon III by attempting a coup de force, but their attempt to seize arms at the fire station on the Boulevard de la Villette failed. On hearing of the defeat at Sedan, where Napoleon was taken prisoner, Palikao fled to Belgium. The revolution of 4 September broke out in Paris.

After the collapse of the Empire, the terrain of class struggle was thus cleared of Bonapartism, whose function since 1851 had been precisely to prevent the clash between the bourgeoisie and the proletariat. In Paris, on 4 September, revolution broke out: the people of Paris, led by the internationalists, the Proudhonian socialists and above all the Blanquists, rose up in revolt and, overthrowing the barricades of the National Guards placed in front of the Legislative Assembly, entered the room where the Blanquist Granger ordered the deputies to decree the fall of the Empire and the proclamation of the Republic. This is the rehearsal of the scene from February 1848 during which the Second Republic was imposed by Raspail at the head of the armed people. Gambetta, despite the opposition of the legislature and under pressure from Parisians, announced the emperor's forfeiture. A little later at the Town Hall, with Jules Favre and Jules Ferry and other republican deputies, he proclaimed the Republic. A national defense government is established, composed of 11 deputies from Paris. Despite the disaster in Sedan and while Bazaine's army is locked up in Metz, the government refuses defeat and decides to reconstitute an army.

This government included moderate republicans (Jules Ferry, Jules Favre, Léon Gambetta, Ernest Picard), the far-left deputy Henri Rochefort, Jules Simon, and had General Trochu, military governor of the city, as president. Adolphe Thiers (1797–1877), one of the historical leaders of the Orléanist right, refused to take part in this government.

Gambetta is Minister of War and Interior. The Breton general and count de Kératry was appointed prefect of police; he resigned quickly and left Paris in a balloon to take command of the army of Brittany (sad episode of the Conlie camp near Le Mans) at the request of Gambetta, who had also left in October to organize armies in the provinces, and above all to oppose any revolutionary movement. The official proclamations of Trochu and Favre were in the direction of a resistance to the bitter end against the invader, but Trochu, well aware that the greatest enemy remained the Parisian proletariat, made the 40,000 men of Vinoy's army enter Paris. The government having chosen to remain in Paris, a delegation was sent to Tours to coordinate the action in the provinces under the orders of Adolphe Crémieux, Minister of Justice. On 15 September, Adolphe Thiers was mandated and sent on a mission to European capitals to seek support against Prussia.

As in 1830 and 1848, the province followed; Lyon even preceded Paris by proclaiming the Republic a few hours ahead of time.

Moderate Republicans distrust the working class

If the proletariat of '48, blinded by illusions of brotherhood, allowed itself to be stripped of the power which was nevertheless its due, it was not exactly the same for the proletariat of 1870: it handed over power to the representatives in place, but because it could not do otherwise, as Marx explains in the first chapter of *The Civil War*.... The enemy was at the gates, the imperial armies were either locked up without recourse in Metz or imprisoned in Germany; the real leaders of the working class were still in the Bonapartist prisons. At this extreme, the people allowed the Parisian deputies of the former legislature to form a "government of national defense"; *they allowed it on the express condition that this seizure of power would be exercised solely for the purposes of national defense;*

and they allowed it all the more willingly, in order to ensure defense during the siege of Paris, when all Parisians in a position to bear arms joined the National Guard, so that the workers now constituted the great majority.

But Thiers and his friends want peace as soon as possible for fear of the revolution!

The Siege of Paris

On 18 September 1870, the German armies from Sedan, which had met no resistance, stood in front of Paris and threatened it with a siege. On the following days, they dispersed the French troops on the Chatillon plateau, also surrounding the town from the south where it was less defended by the 16 forts distributed over a perimeter of 53 km. The encirclement of Paris and the external forts and redoubts was thus completed. The German armies stand at a distance within a radius of 10 to 20 km and stretch out in a long cordon of about a hundred kms. But this encirclement does not exceed 300 men per km, which would make it possible to break the noose. The German command with Bismarck and Kaiser Wilhelm moved to Versailles on 19 September. At the beginning, it had 672 cannons, 150,000 men (Prussians, Saxons, Baden, Würtemburgers, Bavarians), but this figure increased with the liberation of the siege troops (Metz, Toul, Strasbourg) to reach 400,000 men. The transport of heavy artillery did not begin until the end of November, once the rail routes had been checked. A German administration of the occupied territories was set up between mid-September and mid-October with three zones of occupation (Lorraine, Champagne, Nord and Ile de France). On the French side, Paris had 80,000 soldiers of the army of the line, 14,000 sailors, 20,000 special corps (train, gendarmerie, customs officers...) The mobile national guard, essentially raised in the departments, comprised 100,000 men who were poorly supervised and little trained. The sedentary national guard will rise to 300,000 hastily armed and undisciplined Parisian men. Thus Paris prepared for the struggle with 540,000 rifles, including 200,000 chassepots—the best rifle of the time—2,600 cannons; 230 other pieces would be manufactured during the siege. 500,000 men were mobilized in Paris and for its external defenses, forts and redoubts, against 180,000 German soldiers at the beginning. Trochu will either leave these forces inactive or organize disastrous operations. And instead of regrouping the troops, he maintained three formations: the active army, the mobile troops and the armed civilians, i.e. the sedentary National Guard, which he left without military training. Some groups of *franc tireurs* or "partisans" intervene in front of the line of forts. Other groups of franc tireurs will carry out guerrilla actions (sabotage of railways, tunnels and bridges) aided by popular resistance in the occupied zones. These phenomena of franc tireurs will irritate the German armies who will retaliate with requisitions and other reprisals (events of Chateaudun in October 70). The fall of Napoleon, according to Bismarck and William I, should have been the aim of this war; obviously it was not. The conflict continued, revealing Bismarckian imperialism: it was a war directed against the French people, and therefore against its insurgent proletariat in Paris and elsewhere. The Prussian junkers therefore levied heavy taxes in the occupied French cities and departments; they mercilessly shot the resistance fighters (francs-tireurs), plundered abandoned houses, requisitioned with ruthless rigour.

The siege of Paris thus began on 19 September and inaugurated the period that Victor Hugo would call "the terrible year". The siege will be hard on the population, which will experience famine, a tripled mortality rate, but which will resist heroically.

Only the strong patriotic feeling and the need to defend the Fatherland united the revolutionary elements to this government; so, in the first days after 4 September, the internationalists and the delegates of the trade union chambers came to Gambetta at the Town Hall to ask the government to organize the defense, and Blanqui, in his newspaper *La Patrie en danger*, supported the government. But Marx and Engels were under no illusions from the start. In his letter of 7 September 1870, Engels wrote to Marx: "The entire republic, like its pacific origin, has been a complete farce up to now…The Orleanists have the real power: Trochu the military command and Kératry the police; the gentlemen of the *gauche* have the hot-air portfolios" (M-E, XLIV, 67).

This government had promised the workers the immediate elections of the Commune, but it did not keep its word. And very quickly it turned out that it was more afraid of the working class, which had given it power, than of the Prussian enemy. "In this conflict between national duty and class interest, the Government of National Defence did not hesitate one moment to turn into a Government of National Defection." (M-E, XXII, 311).

b. The government of national defection

"Paris, however, was not to be defended without arming its working class, organizing them into an effective force, and training their ranks by the war itself. But Paris armed was the Revolution armed. A victory of Paris over the Prussian aggressor would have been a victory of the French workman over the French capitalist and his State parasites" (M-E, XXII, 311).

While Thiers went around the European courts begging for their intervention, Jules Favre confessed in a letter to Gambetta that what they were defending themselves against were not Prussian soldiers, but workers from Paris (quoted in *The Civil War...*). Moreover Trochu, on the evening of 4 September, harangued the mayors of Paris, saying that the city was in no condition to withstand a siege against the Prussian army; his plan was already the capitulation of Paris, but instead of informing the people of Paris, "they resolved to cure them of their heroic madness". And this was the good farce of the defense which ended with the capitulation of 23 January 1871. Thus, the government did not take seriously the preparations for the defense, nor the operations of the siege: the earthworks were dragged out, the sorties were poorly organized and without precise objectives.

Jules Favre meets Bismarck in Ferrières, on September 19th and 20th. General Ducroc convinced Trochu to take over the Châtillon redoubt from the Prussians. As the means committed were insufficient, Ducroc had to withdraw!

In any case Von Moltke and Bismarck decided to avoid exposing their troops and are counting on weariness and hunger to obtain the capitulation of Paris.

In the Second Address of the IWMA of 9 September 1870, Marx had warned the French workers as follows: "The Orleanists have seized the strongholds of the army and the police, while to the professed Republicans have fallen the talking departments. Some of their first acts go far to show that they have inherited from the Empire, not only ruins, but also its dread of the working class." (M-E, XXII, 269)

In fact, the ruling classes knew very well that the armed working class would wage a revolutionary war that would lead to questioning the very existence of the bourgeoisie; the latter therefore preferred to make a pact with the enemy in order to crush the communist revolution that the Parisian proletariat represented: "the national Governments are *one* as against the proletariate!" (M-E, XXII, 354)

But in October, faced with the inefficiency of their government, popular unrest resumed...

3. THE REVOLUTION IN PROGRESS

a. The proletariat organizes itself

As of September 5, a *vigilance committee* is appointed at public meetings for each borough. The revolutionary forces represented by the internationalists, the Blanquists and the republicans thus sought to organize a defense. Lissagaray recounts:

> On 5 September, wanting to centralize the forces of the Action Party for the defense and maintenance of the Republic, they had invited public meetings to appoint in each district a Vigilance Committee responsible for monitoring the mayors and receiving complaints. Each committee was to appoint four delegates, the total number of delegates would be a Central Committee of the 20 districts. This tumultuous mode of election had produced a committee composed of workers, employees and writers known in the revolutionary movements and meetings of recent years. It had been set up in the room in the rue de la Corderie lent by the International and the Federation of Trade Union Chambers.

Although the Committee kept its autonomy and was not confused with the International or with the representatives of the trade union chambers, the "Corderie" had become the heart of revolutionary Paris, acting as a link between the tendencies. Some members of the Committee, Lefrançais, Malon, Pindy, were part of the International. Gabriel Ranvier was a Blanquist, Millière represented the republican intellectuals. From 15 September, this Committee affirmed its program: election of the municipalities, the police handed over to them, the election and responsibility of all magistrates, the absolute right of press, of meeting, of association, the expropriation of all basic necessities, the arming of all citizens, the sending of commissioners to monitor the province.

In addition, the "red" clubs where all the problems were discussed multiplied; and the National Guard, composed before the conflict of about sixty men loyal to the Empire, now included a *majority of workers* who enlisted to defend Paris, thus increasing the number of men to more than 200,000.

b. The Commune of 1792 is claimed as of 22 September.

Faced with the inertia of the government, which postponed the elections and no longer mentioned the word "Republic" in its official texts, and the successive failures of the poorly organized exits from Paris, Paris became agitated.

On 22 September, delegates from the 20 borough committee and representatives of the National Guard demanded elections for the Commune. "May the Commune, as in 1792, save the city and France", exclaimed Lissagaray.

On 30 September, on the news of the capitulation of Strasbourg, the revolutionary republicans (who oppose the parliamentary republicans who accept that the Republic is a political form of the old State), led by Blanquists and internationalist leaders, begin their agitation, especially among the National Guards.

On 5 October, the scholar Gustave Paul Flourens, commander of a defense sector, came down from the hill of Belleville in Paris with his 10 battalions of national guards to demand arms, a mass mobilization, exits to unblock Paris from the Prussian siege, the cleansing of the Bonapartist personnel still in place, and the immediate elections of the Commune. Jules Ferry, secretary of the government, refused on 9 October to receive another delegation of workers battalions.

The government is also seeking to arrest Flourens and Blanqui!

c. The October 30 Uprising

Thiers, charged by the government to find support from other European countries, comes back disappointed.

The surrender without fighting in Metz of the army of the Rhine commanded by General Bazaine, a Bonapartist, on October 27, is proof of the treason of the government of bourgeois counter-revolution. Here is how Bazaine begged for an armistice: "Society is threatened by a violent party…my army is destined to be the safeguard of society; it is the only force that can tame anarchy…It would offer Prussia, by effect of this action, a guarantee of pledges that Prussia could claim, it would contribute to the coming of a regular power" (Bourdin, *La Commune de Paris*).

The repercussions of the fall of Metz soon became apparent with the memorable day of October 30th.

The workers organized among others in the National Guard rose up and took prisoner almost all the government in the Town Hall, because, with the surrender of Metz, "there is no higher treason in history" (Lissagaray). Blanqui and his supporters took the lead. The new power included Blanqui, Delescluze, Flourens, Félix Pyat, and also Ranvier, Dorian, V. Hugo, Rochefort, Vaillant, Louis Blanc and Raspail. But it negotiated, and on the evening of the 31st it released its prisoners who promised elections to the Commune and the non pursuit of the insurgents. Rochefort resigned from the government on 1 November.

Engels describes the outcome of the uprising as follows: "Treachery, the government's direct breach of its undertakings, and the intervention of some petty-bourgeois battalions set them free again, and in order not to occasion the outbreak of civil war inside a city besieged by a foreign military power, the former government was left in office" (M-E, XXVII, 183).

And Marx, in the first draft of *The Civil War…* notes:

> The different movements at Paris in the beginning of October aimed at the establishment of the Commune, as a measure of defence against the Foreign invasion, as the realisation of the rise of the 4th of September. Its establishment by the movement of the 31 October failed only because Blanqui, Flourens and the other then leaders of the movement believed in the gens de paroles who had given their parole d'honneur to abdicate and make room to a Commune freely elected by all the arrondissements of Paris. It failed because they saved the lives of those men so eager for the assassination of their saviours. Having allowed Trochu and Ferry to escape, they [were] surprised then by Trochu's Bretons… The victorious establishment at Paris of the Commune in the beginning of November 1870 (then already initiated in the great cities of the country and sure to be imitated all over France)…would have altogether changed the character of the war. It would have become the war of republican France, hoisting the flag of the social Revolution of the 19th century, against Prussia, the banner bearer of the conquest and counterrevolution By the escamotage of the Commune on October 31, the Jules Favre and Co secured the capitulation of France to Prussia and initiated the present civil war (M-E, XXII, 480-481).

d. The farce of the plebiscite of 3 November

On 3 November, the government of National Defense, strongly shaken by the revolutionary actions of 30 October, hastily organized a vote. In a besieged

Paris, in the midst of a climate of fear and constraint, and under the action of intense demagogic propaganda (the government denounced the movement of 30 October as a conspiracy with the Prussians; it appointed Clément Thomas commander of the National Guard and called on the middle classes to frighten the workers battalions), a plebiscite was launched on the question of whether or not the population agreed to maintain the powers of the government.

From the plebiscite 557,000 yes's and 62,000 no's resulted. Lissagaray comments as follows: *"How could 60,000 clairvoyants (...) never govern opinion? They were divided into 100 currents (...) Delescluze and Blanqui lived in an exclusive circle of friends or supporters. Félix Pyat (...) only came in handy to save his own skin. The other Ledru-Rollin, Louis Blanc, Schoelcher, etc..., the hope of the Republicans under the Empire, had returned from exile in a state of stagnation (...) The radicals, concerned about their future, were not going to compromise themselves in the Committee of the 20 districts (...) I can see at the Corderie the lost children of the petty bourgeoisie who hold the pen or speak out (...) All is silent. Except in the suburbs, Paris is a patient room where nobody dares say a word"*.

e. Open repression begins

On 5 November, elections for mayors and deputies were held in Paris, resulting in 12 mayorships favourable to the government and 8 acquired from supporters of the Commune, including Delescluze in the 19th arrondissement and Ranvier, Millière and Flourens in the 20th, as well as in the 11th and 18th arrondissements. Faced with these successes of the revolutionaries, the government went on the attack and issued arrest warrants against the popular leaders. Flourens is thus arrested and will only be freed on 21 January by the national guards.

From November to January, the French armies went from defeat to defeat; on 28 November, General Ducrot, after having exposed the National Guards during an outing outside Paris to useless sacrifices, ordered the retreat.

Living conditions in Paris during the winter of '70–71 were very difficult due to the lack of supplies.

f. The armistice of 28 January 1871

On 6 January, the Central Committee of the 20 districts put up the "red poster": "Place au peuple, place à la Commune", written in large part by Jules Vallès, but also by Tridon, Vaillant, and which also called for the resignation of the government and the continuation of the war. On 9 January, the Committee once again rose up against the capitulators.

To cool the ardour of the National Guard, Trochu launches a suicide sortie towards Buzenval (towards Rueil Malmaison east of Paris) on January 19. Three columns are led by Generals Vinoy, Bellemare and Ducrot. It was a hecatomb of 5,000 dead that discouraged any other attempt to get out.

After the useless and bloody exit of Buzenval on 19th January, General Trochu is replaced by General Vinoy; but the population is exasperated. On the evening of the 21st, members of the clubs and vigilance committees invited the national guards to come armed to the square in front of the town hall, while revolutionaries freed Flourens and other prisoners arrested on 31st October 1870. On the 22nd, the Republican Alliance sent a delegation to the town hall, which was dismissed. A demonstration led by the Blanquists takes place the same day and is a new failure; from the fortified town hall, furnished with Breton mobiles, a shooting breaks out, which sweeps the square and leaves 30 dead. Delescluze is arrested, the clubs are closed, the republican newspapers are suppressed. The government of National Defense was in control of the situation and could accomplish the plan it had been planning since the beginning of the siege: to stop the resistance and hand Paris over to the Prussians.

On January 28, 1871, using famine as a pretext, Jules Favre negotiated an armistice at Versailles (the government did not yet dare to sign the peace agreement); and this came ten days after the meeting of the States of northern and southern Germany which had offered the imperial crown to William of Prussia at Versailles. The French army must give back its cannons...

The news of the surrender was like a blow on the nape of the neck for the Parisians; the stunned city hardly moved. To shake the masses, it took the entry of the Germans into Paris, the cowardly and hasty capitulation of the bourgeoisie.

g. Bismarck, accomplice of the French government

If he remained cautious, Bismarck did not want to finish with Paris any less. With the capitulation, the French government opened the civil war that it was now going to start with the aid of Prussia, against the Republic, against Paris and above all against the Revolution in progress. The trap was set in the very clauses of the capitulation. Bismarck demanded the national election of an Assembly within 8 days, which was to decide between peace and war. Marx comments on this clause: "At that time above one-third of the territory was in the hands of the enemy, the capital was cut off from the provinces, all communications were disorganized. To elect under such circumstances a real representation of France was impossible, unless ample time were given for preparation.

In view of this, the capitulation stipulated that a National Assembly must be elected within eight days; so that in many parts of France the news of the impending election arrived on its eve only" (M-E, XXII, 318).

Gambetta, opposed to the capitulation, resigned from the government (part of the government being in Bordeaux) in February. Indeed, on 31 January, the government had promulgated a decree depriving of the right to vote the personalities who had held high positions in the Bonapartist government, in view of the elections for the Assembly. Bismarck protested against this decree, and the government in Paris, "prisoner of Bismarck", annulled it. Gambetta then resigned.

4. THE COUNTER-REVOLUTION IS UNLEASHED

a. Elections for the Assembly of Rural People on 6 February 1871

Thiers, even before the secret of the armistice had been revealed in Paris, had gone on an electoral tour through the *départements* to galvanise and remind people of the Legitimist Party, which from then on was to take the place of the Bonapartists, who were no longer tolerated, alongside the Orléanists. A new chamber was needed to negotiate peace!

The elections gave a monarchist majority: out of 750 deputies, 450 monarchists composed of aristocrats, the Orleans upper bourgeoisie and legitimist gentry, who represented above all the large landed property, hence its name "Assembly of rural people", as proclaimed by the radical deputy from Marseille, Gaston Crémieux, from the stands during the session of 13 February in Bordeaux.

In Paris, out of 43 elected representatives, 6 are partisans of capitulation (Thiers who will be elected in thirteen departments, and Jules Favre obviously). Lissagaray comments: "The list that came out on 6 February was a harlequin of all republican shades and all political... Louis Blanc, who all the committees supported except the Corderie, led the way with 216,000 votes, followed by Victor Hugo, Gambetta, Garibaldi. Delescluze received 154,000 votes. Millières was elected... The vigilant sentinel who had always shown sagacity throughout the siege, Blanqui, found only 52,000 votes—roughly the opponents of the plebiscite—while Félix Pyat received 145,000 for his "Combat" blarneys...This confused ballot at least attested to the republican idea."

Representatives of the International and the Committee of the 20 districts, such as Tolain, Malon, Gambon, were also elected.

b. The government hands France over to the Prussians

With the capitulation of 28 January, the mask of the imposture of the bourgeoisie was finally thrown off. Marx notes, in *The Civil War...*: "With the true heroism of utter self-debasement, the Government of National Defence, in their capitulation, came out as the Government of France by Bismarck's prisoners." (M-E, XXII, 313)

Indeed, the bourgeoisie was in a hurry to finish off the revolution; as they counted on Bismarck to help them, they threw themselves at his feet ignobly and, without discussing the price honorably, delivered France to the Prussian winner.

On 13th February, the assembly of rural people from Tours, which had passed through Bordeaux, met. Garibaldi had to renounce his mandate because of his Italian nationality, and he was booed by the monarchist majority of the deputies. The debates were very agitated between a republican minority and a monarchist majority. On the 17th, it elected as head of government Adolphe Thiers, "the most consummate intellectual expression of their own class-corruption" (M-E, XXII, 314), head of the executive power. The latter chose his ministers, who were just as bad as he was: Jules Favre, Picard, Dufaure, Jules Simon, Pouyer-Quertier. Marx sarcastically depicts in *The Civil War...* the little hidden vices of each of these sad characters.

On 26 February, the preliminaries for peace are signed in Versailles between Thiers, Favre and Bismarck; the conditions are draconian for France: Bismarck extorted from France the fabulous sum of 5 billion gold francs; he demanded the maintenance of half a million of his soldiers on French soil and interest at 5% on overdue payments; the Prussians were to return to Paris in groups of 30,000 men from 3 March and occupy the Champs Elysées; the eastern forts were to be occupied until the first 500 million had been paid and the eastern departments until the final payment was made. Finally, Bismarck snatched Alsace minus Belfort from France, and a third of Germanic Lorraine with Metz and Strasbourg to incorporate them into Germany. That same day, the Parisians took the garrison's cannons and installed them in Belleville and Montmartre!

Engels writes:

> Paris surrendered, it paid a contribution of 200 millions; the
> forts were handed over to the Prussians; the garrison laid

down its arms before the victors and delivered up its field guns; the cannons on the wall around Paris were taken off their gun carriages; all means of resistance belonging to the state were handed over piece by piece. But the actual defenders of Paris, the National Guard, the armed Parisians, remained untouched, for nobody expected them to give up their arms, either their rifles or their cannons; and so that it would be known to the whole world that the victorious German army had respectfully stopped before the armed people of Paris, the victors did not enter Paris, but were content to be allowed to occupy for three days the Champs Elysées, a public park, protected, guarded and enclosed on all sides by the sentries of the Parisians! No German soldier set foot in Paris City Hall or stepped on the boulevards, and the few that were admitted to the Louvre to admire the art treasures there had to ask for permission... France was defeated, Paris starved, but the Parisian people had by their glorious past ensured respect for themselves, so that no victor dared to demand their disarmament, no one had the courage to enter their homes... Bismarck appeared for the first time as an independent politician, who was no longer implementing in his own way a programme dictated from outside, but translating into action the products of his own brain, thereby committing his first enormous blunder" (M-E, XXVI, 490-491).

Engels alludes to the international consequences of this annexation, which we will develop further on.

Thiers told the Assembly that peace preliminaries should be agreed on the spot, without even the honors of a parliamentary debate. Marx commented: "... as the only condition on which Prussia would permit them to open the war against the Republic and Paris, its stronghold. The counter-revolution had, in fact, no time to lose." (M-E, XXII, 319)

On 1 March, the Assembly ratified the treaty despite the desperate protest of the Alsatian and Lorraine deputies, by 546 votes to 107. Félix Pyat, Malon and Rochefort resigned.

The Frankfurt Peace Treaty signed on 10 May 1871 officially ended the Franco-Prussian war. Napoleon III went into exile in Great Britain with his family.

The political outcome of this war is fundamental. France lost Alsace and Lorraine (annexed in the 18th century). The four southern German States saw the end of their existence in favor of Prussia. Relations between Germany, which had become a dangerous power, and Russia deteriorated and France moved closer to Russia. Germany will thus be surrounded by the hostility of France, Russia and England, which will inevitably lead to the 1914-18 confrontation planned by Engels.

Freed from the external war, the Assembly could now take care of Paris.

c. Heavy toll of the Franco-German war

From mid-July 1870 to January 1871

265,000 French soldiers in the Army of the Rhine clashed with 500,000 Prussian soldiers, plus 300,000 soldiers from the southern German States – a total of 800,000 soldiers!

Human losses are estimated at 44,000 dead in the German ranks (14% of the total), half of whom were ill, 128,000 wounded and 100,000 sick. On the French side, 139,000 died (in combat or through illness), 143,000 were wounded and 320,000 sick. These figures include civilians affected by the bombing and famine, and the tragedies of the Coulie camp of Bretons. Smallpox decimated the ranks of both armies, but Prussians who knew the effectiveness of the smallpox vaccine had far fewer losses from the disease (8,500 Prussians infected and 450 dead, 125,000 French infected and 23,500 dead!).

This war will mark a decisive change in military tactics. The cavalry, which had dominated battles for centuries, no longer had a role to play because of the precision of rifles such as the French chassepot and the use of percussion shells. Heavy artillery is decisive and now finishes the battle.

d. Counter-revolution has no time to lose

Let us continue with Marx (M-E, XXII, 319):

> The counter-revolution had, in fact, no time to lose. The Second Empire had more than doubled the national debt, and plunged all the large towns into heavy municipal debts. The war had fearfully swelled the liabilities, and mercilessly ravaged the resources of the nation. To complete the ruin, the Prussian Shylock was demanding... his indemnity of five milliards... Who was to pay the bill? It was only by the violent overthrow of the

Republic that the appropriators of wealth could hope to shift on to the shoulders of its producers the cost of a war which they, the appropriators, had themselves originated. Thus, the immense ruin of France spurred on these patriotic representatives of land and capital, under the very eyes and patronage of the invader, to graft upon the foreign war a civil war—a slaveholders' rebellion. There stood in the way of this conspiracy one great obstacle—Paris. To disarm Paris was the first condition of success.

Paris was first summoned by Thiers to surrender; on 6 March, an attempt to remove the Paris guns parked in Luxembourg was a failure.

Then Paris was harassed by the frenetic anti-Republican demonstrations of the Assemblée des ruraux and by the equivocal declarations of Thiers himself on the legal status of the Republic; by the threat to decapitate and decapitalize Paris (on 10 March, the Assembly chose Versailles and not Paris as its place of residence); by the appointment of Orléanist ambassadors; by the Dufaure laws on commercial deadlines and rents which ruined Parisian trade and industry. Lissagaray, referring to the Dufaure laws, wrote: "300,000 workers, shopkeepers, tailors, small manufacturers and merchants who had spent their savings during the siege and earned nothing yet were thrown at the mercy of the landlord and bankruptcy". And further on: "What the perils of the siege had failed to achieve, the Assembly did: the union of the petty bourgeoisie with the proletariat".

In addition, the Pouyer-Quertier tax on each copy of all publications, the death sentences against Blanqui and Flourens because of the insurrection of 30 October (Blanqui was arrested on 17 March in the Lot, where he was resting), the suppression of republican newspapers, the renewal proclaimed by Palikao of the state of siege abolished on 4 September, the suppression of the indemnity granted to the national guards; and finally the appointment of Vinoy, involved in the 18th Brumaire coup, as governor of Paris, that of Valentin, the gendarme of the Empire, as prefect of police, that of Burelles de Paladine, the Jesuit general, as commander of the national guard in place of Clément Thomas, who had preferred to resign... Thiers had handed Paris over to the tender solicitude of this triumvirate. And these gentlemen of the government were all the more in a hurry, as Marx always stressed, in *The Civil War...*, that they had contracted a loan of 2 billion, with an enormous bribe for each of them, which was not to be paid, loan and bribes, until after the "pacification" of Paris. Marx concluded:

"At all events, there must have been something very pressing in the matter, for Thiers and Jules Favre, in the name of the majority of the Bordeaux Assembly, unblushingly solicited the immediate occupation of Paris by Prussian troops. Such, however, was not the game of Bismarck..." (M-E, XXII, 320).

5. REVOLUTIONARY PARIS RISES UP

a. Continuing the struggle

It is known that at the beginning of September Paris had already appointed vigilance committees responsible for organizing the defense and supply of the working class districts. During the siege, the National Guard had been increasingly reinforced in numbers and equipment with weapons and cannons acquired by subscription; it now constituted an army of more than 200,000 men divided into 260 battalions, equipped with 450,000 rifles, 2,000 cannons and their supplies (according to Talès). Thiers asked Paris to lay down its arms under a pretext that was the most blatant lie, namely that the artillery of the National Guard belonged to the State; this artillery had been officially recognized as the private property of the National Guard in the capitulation of 28 January and as such had been exempted from the general surrender. But the revolution did not want to lay down its arms; it still wanted to defend Paris and France.

Marx, in the first draft of *The Civil War...*, writes:

> Thus also the rising of all living Paris... against the government of Defence does not date from the 18th of March, although it conquered on that day its first victory against the conspirators, it dates from the 28 January, from the very day of the capitulation. The National Guard—that is all the armed manhood of Paris—organized itself and really ruled Paris from that day, independently of the usurpatory government of the capitulards 165 installed by the grace of Bismarck. It refused to deliver its arms and artillery, which was its property and only left them in the capitulation because its property. It was not the magnanimity of Jules Favre that saved these arms from Bismarck, but the readiness of armed Paris to fight for its arms against Jules Favre and Bismarck. (M-E, XXII, 482).

b. The National Guard Federation on February 24th

Lissagaray tells us that towards the end of January some Republicans tried to group the National Guards for electoral purposes. A large meeting had first taken place at the Cirque d'Hiver under the chairmanship of a merchant, Courty. A second meeting was held on 15 February in the Vauxhall theatre, but no further thought was given to elections. Only one thought occupied all hearts: the union of the Parisian forces against the rural triumphant for the *defense of the Republic*. The idea of a federation came out of the meeting, and it was decided that the battalions would be grouped around a Central Committee (CC). A commission was given the task of drawing up the statutes of the new organization, i.e. the federation of the companies with the creation of a central committee made up of delegates from the different companies.

Each district represented in the room—18 out of 20—appointed a commissioner for this committee on the spot. "Who are they? The agitators at headquarters, the socialists of the Corderie, the famous writers? None of them. There were no names of bourgeois renown among the elected officials. The commissioners are petty bourgeois, shopkeepers, employees, foreigners to all the coteries, up to that point even to politics for the most part"(Lissagaray, *Histoire de la Commune de Paris 1871*).

Among the CC, we already find Georges Arnold (architect of the city of Paris), André Alavoine (typographer, Blanquist, he will take care of the national printing house), Gaston Da Costa (Blanquist student), future communards. Their president, the merchant Courty, is a moderate republican.

On 24 February, the General Assembly of 2,000 delegates of the National Guards at the Vauxhall approves these statutes, votes in favor of abolishing the "national armies" and undertakes to intervene if the Prussians enter Paris as provided for in the treaty. Demonstrations take place in Paris, shouting "Vive la République"(Long live the Republic!). The atmosphere is therefore explosive.

On 27 February, a few days before the entry of the Prussians provided for in the treaty, the battalions of the National Guard decided to go and get the 237 cannons and machine guns paid for by the Paris subscriptions and which had been treacherously abandoned by the capitulators in the districts that the Prussians were to occupy (in the parks of Passy, the Place Wagram, the Ranelagh) . These cannons were transported to the east of Paris, Montmartre, Belleville, Ménilmontant, la Villette, Place des Vosges and the Italian Barrier, while armed groups waited on the Champs Elysées and Avenue de la Grande Armée for the arrival of the Prussians. On the 28th, a meeting of battalion chiefs and delegates of the military committees chaired by Jules Bergeret wanted to implement the decisions of the 24th, i.e. to prevent the entry of the Prussians, but the members of the commission, which acted like a central committee, dissuaded them from doing so. On the morning of the 28th, the three groups of the Place de la Corderie—the General Council of the Paris International, the Federation of Trade Union Chambers and the CC of the 20 districts—had posted a manifesto warning the workers to abstain, but these three disorganized and reduced groups had little audience compared with the representatives of the armed mass.

On 1 March, the Chamber ratified the preliminaries of peace, despite the protest of the Alsatian and Lorraine deputies, by 546 votes to 107; the Prussians entered the beautiful districts: 30,000 marched silently under the eye of the insurgents, and Emperor William renounced his visit. They left Paris on the 2nd. The city could not forget the outrage, and the news from the Bordeaux Assembly only made it more excited (with the bills on rents, the vote on the conditions of peace, etc.).

On March 3, the assembly of delegates from 200 battalions votes on the statutes of the Republican Federation of the National Guard. The National Guard becomes the Republican Federation and the National Guards "federated". It appoints an executive commission that must specify the role of the central committee and, in the meantime, must concentrate the powers of the National Guard. It includes Jules Bergeret, Auguste Viard (commerce employee), Jean Louis Pindy (carpenter, member of the IWMA), Eugène Varlin (member of the IWMA), Jacques Louis Durand (cobbler).

On 8 March, Victor Hugo resigned in the middle of the Assembly session, after another incident involving Garibaldi. On March 10, the Assembly votes on its transfer to Versailles. On the same day, Jules Favres wrote to Thiers: "We are determined to put an end to the redoubts of Montmartre and Belleville" (Louise Michel, *La Commune, histoire et souvenirs*). The Chamber decided to suspend the pay of the National Guards and the moratorium on rents, a measure which had been taken to offset the effects of the siege and the economic blockade. Georges Clémenceau, doctor to the poor and mayor of Montmartre since September 1870, tried in vain to reconcile Paris and Versailles. Thiers moved to Paris on 16 March to "pacify" the city.

c. The People's Government of Paris

On 13 March, the Federation of the National Guard is ratified by 215 battalions out of 270, and elects its delegates. Marx, in the first draft of *The Civil War...* (M-E, XXII, 483), writes: "On its existing military organization it grafted a political federation according to a very simple plan. It was the alliance of all the National Guards put in connection the one with the other by the delegates of each company, appointing in their turn the delegates of the battalions, who in their turn appointed general delegates, generals of legions, who were to represent an arrondissement and to cooperate with the delegates of the 19 other arrondissements. Those 20 delegates, chosen by the majority of the battalions of the National Guard, composed the Central Committee."

The Central Committee (CC) would sit at Corderie, this revolutionary center, in the premises already occupied by the General Council of the Paris section of the International (which on the whole remained hesitant about its participation in this CC; four members would nevertheless be part of it), the Federation of Trade Union Chambers, and the CC of the 20 districts. Who are the members of the CC? Lissagaray gives us the account of the election session:

> Garibaldi was acclaimed Chief General of the National Guard. A speaker, Lullier, a former naval officer, excited the assembly... He was appointed commander of the artillery. The names of the elected members of the CC were then announced—about thirty; several districts had not yet voted. It is the regular CC, the one that will enter the Town Hall. Many of the elected members belonged to the previous committee. The others were equally obscure, from all strata of the people, known only to the family councils or their battalions. The men in the limelight had not run for office. The Corderie, the Blanquists too, did not want to admit that this federation, this Committee, these unknown people were a force. They will not work, it is true, for a program whatsoever. The CC is not the head of a party current; it has no ideals to produce. A very simple idea, to defend the republic from the monarchy, was the only one that could bring together so many battalions. The National Guard is formed as an insurance company against a coup d'état; the CC is the sentinel, that is all.

Among the members of the CC are four internationalists (E.Varlin, Assi, Alavoine, Jules Babick), and others such as Jourdes, Fleury, Ranvier, Bergeret, Eudes, Duval, Lullier, Brunel, E.Moreau, etc...

This CC therefore acted like the people's government of the capital; it was recognized by all neighborhood committees; the committee of the *rue des Rosiers* (18th arrondissement), the most important of the committees because of its location and the number of its cannons, initially treated on an equal footing with the CC, to which it did not send delegates until very late. Engels speaks of the CC as follows (presentation on the Commune to the General Council of March 21, 1871; M-E, XXII, 586): "None of the men of the Central Committee were known to fame, there were no Felix Pyats and men of that stamp in it, but they were well known among the working class. There were four members of the International in the Committee. The Commune was to be elected the next day. They had announced that the liberty of the press should be respected but not the rotten Bonapartist press. The most important resolution passed was that the preliminaries of peace should be respected."

And Marx (M-E, XXII, 525): "From the very day of the capitulation, by which the government of the national defence had disarmed France but reserved to itself a bodyguard of 40,000 troops for the purpose of cowing Paris, Paris stood on the watch…. During the whole interval from the meeting of the National Assembly at Bordeaux to the 18th of March, the Central Committee had been the people's government of the capital, strong enough to persist in its firm attitude of defence despite the provocations of the Assembly, the violent measures of the Executive, and the menacing concentration of troops."

The situation was explosive; the Parisian people were reluctant to start a civil war when the bourgeoisie had already been plotting against them and the Revolution since 4 September. The Prussians did not want to openly help the French bourgeoisie to do its dirty work by occupying Paris; all that was left for the latter to do was to get on with it; so on 18 March it attacked again: disarm Paris, since Paris armed is revolution!

6. MARCH 18: THE ENEMY IS NO LONGER GERMANY BUT THE BOURGEOISIE!

Civil war is declared!

a. The bourgeoisie goes on the attack

Engels comments (M-E, XXVII, 183-184):

> During the war the Paris workers had confined themselves to demanding the vigorous prosecution of the fight. But now, when peace had come after the capitulation of Paris,161 now

Thiers, the new supreme head of the government, was compelled to realise that the rule of the propertied classes—big landowners and capitalists—was in constant danger so long as the workers of Paris had arms in their hands. His first action was an attempt to disarm them. On March 18, he sent troops of the line with orders to rob the National Guard of the artillery belonging to it, which had been constructed during the siege of Paris and had been paid for by public subscription. The attempt failed; Paris mobilised as one man for resistance, and war between Paris and the French Government sitting at Versailles was declared.

We can reconstruct the facts with the help of Lissagaray; Thiers had ordered his troops led by Vinoy to occupy the Buttes Chaumont, Belleville, the Temple, the Bastille, the Town Hall, Montmartre, the Invalides and to take back the cannons parked "in the field of the Poles" (the space on which the Sacré Coeur was to be built in 1873) of Montmartre, with the pretext that these cannons could have been recovered by the Prussians! This was done at three o'clock in the morning without a blow, because only one national guard had been assigned to guard the artillery park. Louise Michel and Dr. Clemenceau, mayor of the 18th century, rushed quickly to treat the wounded guard. But Vinoy had not foreseen the horses to move the cannons, which took time and left the suburbs to wake up. Posters signed by Thiers and his ministers had already been put up on the walls of Paris. Awakened, the population then realized the aggression, reacted immediately, called out the soldiers and gave the alert. The attempt is beaten, with national guards roaming the 18th arrondissement (Montmartre). The troops of General Claude Lecomte, who were to occupy Montmartre, fraternized with the national guards and the crowd. General Lecomte three times asked his soldiers to shoot at the crowd, then insulted them. His soldiers wanted to shoot him, but the National Guards present prevented them from doing so and took Lecomte to Château-Rouge, headquarters of the battalions of the National Guard of Montmartre.

The popular reaction and turnaround is the same in other neighborhoods. At eleven o'clock, the people had defeated the aggression on all points, kept almost all their cannons and won thousands of rifles.

D'Aurelles de Paladine had the national guards called since six o'clock in the morning; 500 to 600 answered.

The morning aggression surprised the CC of the National Guard like all Paris. The vigilance committees and the National Guards stationed in the neighborhood were able to support the defensive reaction of the Parisian people. Thus, Louise Michel and Ferré, members of the vigilance committee of the 18th arrondissement, took part in seizing back the guns of Montmartre. Around 4.30 pm, Clément Thomas, the man of June 1848, was arrested on Rue des Martyrs (in the 18th arrondissement). The soldiers and the crowd, fighting against the national guards who wanted to oppose them, shot General Lecomte, arrested in the morning, and Clément Thomas, "this personal enemy of the working class of Paris", in Rue des Rosiers.

Little by little, the federated battalions took the offensive and occupied the barracks and the national printing works. Thus the CC of the National Guard directs the action, organizes the fighting (gather the battalions, make the troops pass to the side of the National Guard, raise barricades, seize vital points). The federates surrounded the town hall and Brunel's troops took possession of it after the members of the government and the gendarmes had fled.

When he learns of the stampede of his troops and their fraternization with the population, Thiers gives the order to withdraw them to the Champ de Mars. When three battalions of national guards pass in front of the ministry where he has taken refuge, the government thinks it is lost. Thiers, panic-stricken, fled by a concealed staircase and was escorted to Versailles by a squadron. On the evening of 18th March, he gave the order to evacuate Paris to all government services and barracks. He thought of rebuilding an army at Versailles; he even ordered the evacuation of the southern forts that had been returned by the Prussians a fortnight earlier, among them the Mont Valérien, a strategic point in the defense of Paris and Versailles, because Thiers only thought of protecting himself at Versailles. It's a stampede. Unfortunately, the insurgents, "too honest", badly organized and badly directed, did not take advantage of it.

b. The CC governs

"The glorious working men's Revolution of the 18th March took undisputed sway of Paris. The Central Committee was its provisional Government." (M-E, XXII, 322).

In this Paris that is beginning to empty itself of everything that represented the previous regime, the CC, *in spite of itself*, must act as a provisional government, because it is the only one in Paris that can do so.

The "obscure" men who make it up, delegates of popular battalions only known in their districts were surprised by the event, and brought to the Town Hall by the insurrection. They were hesitant, and their first act was to want to hand over power to the Parisian people, that is to say to prepare for the elections to the Commune, which they set for 23 March, but which were later postponed until the 26th. But while waiting for these elections, they governed Paris.

On 19 March, the CC issued two proclamations: it thanked the army for not wanting to "lay a hand on the sound arch of our liberties" and called on Paris and France to "together lay the foundations of an acclaimed republic with all its consequences, the only government that will close forever the era of invasions and civil wars". Consequently, the CC calls on the people of Paris to hold new elections. A similar appeal is addressed to the National Guards. But if it decides "to preserve, in the name of the people" the City Hall, the CC does not consider itself a revolutionary government, but rather the agent who will allow the people to affirm their will through new elections.

Administering Paris

Despite the disarray of the services, life in Paris must continue. Driven by necessity, the CC becomes aware of its role and of the revolution which has just been accomplished on 18 March. It sends delegates to seize the deserted ministries and the various services: the worker Adolphe Assi, a member of the IWMA, received the Town Hall responsibility; the bookbinder, a member of the IWMA, Eugène Varlin, and the notary clerk and accountant François Jourde went to finance; Lucien Combatz was appointed to the Post Office; Ed. Moreau, a Blanquist journalist, was delegated to oversee the Journal Officiel (JO) and the printing works; Duval and Raoul Rigault, also Blanquist journalists, at the Préfecture de Police; Eudes, a Blanquist journalist, at the War Office; the battalion captain of the National Guard, Jules Bergeret, was appointed commander-in-chief of the Paris stronghold.

Members of the International and Blanquists therefore share the important positions.

Lissagaray writes: "In 1831, the proletarians, masters of Lyon for 10 days, had not been able to manage themselves. How much greater the difficulty for Paris... The CC found only malfunctioning cogs. When Versailles had ordered it, most of the employees had abandoned their posts... People came to the CC from everywhere. The district committees provided the staff for the town halls; the petty bourgeoisie lent its experience."

The urgent issue of settling the pay of the National Guardsmen is resolved without violence. Varlin and Jourdes do not dare to force their way into the coffers of the Ministry of Finance, which contain several million francs and whose keys are in Versailles. The CC obtains a credit of one million francs from the governor of the Bank of France.

The CC, considering that the solidarity of the soldiers with the National Guard caused the success of March 18, voted unanimously to abolish the war councils. On the 21st, it suspends the sale of objects hired at the Mount of Piety, extends the deadlines by one month, forbids the owners to dismiss their tenants and grants amnesty to all political prisoners. The CC thus behaves like a provisional government. Varlin, a member of the IWMA, wrote to the Swiss internationalists grouped around Bakunin and Guillaume who saw in 18 March the universal social revolution: "...that it was not an international revolution; that the 18 March movement had no other aim than to demand municipal franchises in Paris and that this aim had been achieved".

There is nothing subversive about such a program and it does not imply military action against Versailles.

Indeed, the CC *basically has a superstitious horror of illegality*, because it is afraid of its consequence: civil war. It constantly preaches moderation, votes unanimously to lift the state of siege, restores freedom of the press. On 23 March, it sets out its program in detail. First of all, it notes the bankruptcy of a power that had led France to defeat and capitulation: "the principle of authority is now powerless to restore order in the streets, to revive work in the workshop, and this powerlessness is its negation". It is therefore necessary to restore order and reorganize work on new bases "which will put an end to class antagonism and ensure social equality". The emancipation of the workers and the communal delegation must ensure the effective control of the people's representatives in charge of social reforms. These social reforms are: the organization of credit, exchange and association, in order to guarantee the worker the integral value of his work, i.e. the disappearance of capitalist profit; free, secular and "integral" education; citizens' freedoms (assembly, association, press); the organization of the police and the army at the communal level. The principle that should govern the whole society is the one that organizes grouping and association. There is therefore a rejection of any authority imposed from outside, whether that of an administrator, a mayor or a prefect, and permanent control of elected representatives.

Making peace with Prussia is tantamount to turning imperialist war into civil war

On 19 March, the CC came out clearly in favor of peace with Prussia: "We declare from now on that we are firmly resolved to enforce its preliminaries in order to safeguard both the salvation of republican France and general peace".

This resolution allowed the transformation of the imperialist war into civil war, as Lenin points out: "The transformation of the present imperialist war into civil war is the only just proletarian watchword, taught by the experience of the Commune" (Lenin, XXI, 160).

The military inertia of the CC

The CC will thus put itself on the defensive. It was going to lift the state of siege to organize the elections, although it had the strength of guns, giving Thiers respite to reorganize the army at Versailles with the help of Bismarck who was there. So while the counter-revolution fled from Paris, the federated battalions tried nothing against it. From the afternoon of 18th March, the CC offered command of the National Guard and thus of the forces of Paris to a former naval commander, Charles Lullier, an alcoholic and braggart, who was already badly rated by his superiors. Whether it was due to treason or incompetence, he proved to be extraordinarily inert.

Far from closing the gates of Paris, he let all the fugitives through (Jules Ferry did not leave until the 18th in the afternoon). He left all the exits open to the army, many of whose soldiers, escaping from the control of their leaders and in contact with the Parisian population, could have passed to the side of the National Guard. He did not immediately occupy the forts abandoned by Thiers' troops: the forts of Ivry, Bicêtre, Montrouge, Vanves and Issy were not occupied until 19 and 20 March; as for the fort of Mont Valérien, a strategic point for defending Paris and then Versailles, he thought about it after Vinoy had finally convinced Thiers to have a sufficient garrison there. On the subject of Mont Valérien, Lissagaray writes:

> For thirty six hours, the impregnable fortress had remained empty. On the evening of the 18th, after the evacuation order sent by M.Thiers, it had only twenty rifles and the Vincennes riflemen interned for having demonstrated at the Bastille.... Deputies and generals begged M.Thiers to have Mont Valérien reoccupied. He stubbornly refused, maintaining that this fort had no strategic value. Finally Vinoy, harassed by the deputies, managed to obtain an order from him, on the 20th, at one o'clock in the morning. A column was dispatched and on the 21st, at noon, a thousand soldiers occupied the fortress...

Finally, Lullier did not order the march on Versailles, then defenseless. In view of his incompetence and his "ambiguous" speeches, he was dismissed on the 22nd. All the fugitives left Paris quietly, and Versailles was organized.

Lullier is replaced by three energetic men: the patriot Brunel, and the two Blanquists Eudes and Duval. They immediately declared: "The time for parliamentarianism is over; we must act and severely punish the enemies of the Republic. Everything that is not with us is against us. Paris wants to be free". Duval called for a march on Versailles, but the majority of the CC preferred to confine itself to preparing for the elections and administering Paris rather than facing the realities of civil war.

The CC therefore relied on the military to reorganize the National Guard and the defense of Paris, unlike Thiers, who kept the direction of operations in hand. For Paris it was the source of bloody setbacks and rivalries with badly organized, tragic outings, despite the devotion of Flourens, Eudes, Duval, La Cécilia, Brunel. These last two, together with Dombrowski, Wroblewsli, all former officers, were the best tacticians of the Commune army. Unfortunately the general organization of defense and strategy entrusted to Lullier, Cluseret and Rossel was disastrous. *Only a determined political leadership would have given the Commune the general staff it lacked.*

Marx wrote in *The Civil War...* : "In their reluctance to continue the civil war opened by Thiers' burglarious attempt on Montmartre, the Central Committee made themselves, this time, guilty of a decisive mistake in not at once marching upon Versailles, then completely helpless, and thus putting an end to the conspiracies of Thiers and his Rurals. Instead of this, the Party of Order was again allowed to try its strength at the ballot-box, on the 26th of March, the day of the election of the Commune" (M-E, XXII, 326).

Bourgeois "resistance"

If the CC as well as the Parisian population, in no way frightened and in an excellent mood, forget the civil war, the bourgeoisie resists angrily.

In Paris, the central districts of the 1st and 2nd arrondissements became the rallying point for all the discontented. The "resistance" included first of all the inconsolable people of the Empire, then the bourgeois and republican intellectuals (the intellectuals of the Latin Quarter, the students of the polytechnic school and the faculty of medicine condemned this CC, without a popular mandate), the elected mayors who claimed to be a legal Commune and were therefore hostile to new municipal elections, the deputies of Paris (including Louis Blanc, Tolain, a member of the IWMA, and Clemenceau), and some battalion leaders. The positions of these resistance fighters vary widely: some are in favor of finding a solution for conciliation between Paris and Versailles, while others are in favor of the Thiers policy and are trying to buy time for the counter-revolution.

Demonstrations took place on the 21st and 22nd March and were aimed at the Place Vendôme, where the headquarters of the National Guard led by Bergeret were installed. On the 21st, the incident was minor, the demonstrators cheered the Assembly and "order" and were dispersed. On the 22nd it was more serious: the demonstrators roughed up the National Guards, a shooting broke out and caused dozens of deaths among the "friends of order", especially the Bonapartists.

The CC has great difficulty in breaking the mayors' resistance to the elections. As early as 19 March, it was announced that the mayors, the deputies of the Seine and battalion chiefs were meeting at the town hall of the 3rd arrondissement and deliberating on the convocation of voters. The CC, conciliatory, let them know that it was ready to negotiate, thus beginning interminable negotiations. Four men were delegated: Varlin, Moreau, Jourde, and Arnold. They were going to give in on all points, including that of handing over the Town Hall to the Parisians. The committee of the 20 boroughs opposed the transaction, and the CC was obliged to disavow its delegates. For their part, the mayors are very badly received by the Versailles Assembly, which does not want conciliation.

The CC postponed the elections to 26 March and occupied the town halls; those in the center resisted. Brunel went there with 600 national guards and, after negotiations, the town halls and the barricaded national guards surrendered and agreed to a deal. In fact, this "resistance", which was not supported by Versailles, would soon collapse.

c. The attitude of internationalists

Apart from Varlin, a member of the CC, the Parisian internationalists have until now kept a great reserve, although the bourgeois press accused them of being responsible for the events.

On 23 March, a joint meeting of the Paris International and the Federal Chamber of Workers' Societies took place. A manifesto, which was to strengthen the CC with "all our moral force", demanded by Frankel, was drawn up in the night, together with a call for communal revolution and a political program. The Parisian internationalists now sought to give the insurrectional movement a program, guidelines: the organization of credit, of exchange; free and secular education; the right of assembly and association; freedom of the press; municipal organization of the police, the armed force, hygiene and statistics.

7. Conclusion
SIGNIFICANCE OF THE REVOLUTIONS OF 4 SEPTEMBER 1870 AND 18 MARCH 1871

...the proletariat undertook two tasks—one of them national and the other of a class character—the liberation of France from the German invasion and the socialist emancipation of the workers from capitalism. This union of two tasks forms a unique feature of the Commune (Lenin, XIII, p.475).

If, from 4 September, the bourgeoisie, conscious of the role to which it was committing itself, shamelessly betrayed its nation with the comedy of defense, the other classes with the proletariat at their head, that is to say the Revolution, bravely rose up against the enemy. It was the Revolution that had taken over the power that had been left vacant and that restored vigor and life to this France that had been decomposed and degenerated by 18 years of Bonapartist parasitism. It regenerated France in two stages: first with the Republic which it imposed on the bourgeoisie on 4 September; the bourgeois government which it left in place *would thus get its legality from workers*. Second, by instituting the Commune, a youthful body built on the ruins of the old State, a putrid corpse from which it rid French society.

In the first draft for *The Civil War...*, Marx writes: "The only legitimate power, therefore, in France is the Revolution itself, centering in Paris. That revolution was not made against Napoleon the little, but against the social and political conditions which engendered the Second Empire, which received their last finish under its sway, and which, as the war with Prussia glaringly revealed, would leave France a cadaver, if they were not superseded by the regenerating powers of the French working class" (M-E, XXII, 451-452).

On 18 March, the Parisian workers revolution took up the glove handed to it by the bourgeoisie, to prevent "the elimination of the Republic that the princes of Orleans and their chargé d'affaires, M. Thiers, were preparing". Marx explains why the Parisians should not back down: "the bourgeois canaille of Versailles were also well aware. Precisely for that reason they presented the

Parisians with the alternative of taking up the fight of succumbing without a struggle. In the latter case, the demoralization of the working class against the capitalist class and its state has entered upon a new phase with the struggle in Paris. Whatever the immediate results may be, a new point of departure of world-historic importance has been gained." (Letter to Kugelmann, 17 April 1871(M-E, XLIV, 136).

The Parisians did not back down. "The traces of the long endured famine still upon their figures, and under the very eye of Prussian bayonets, the Paris working class conquered in one bound the championship of progress" (M-E, XXII, 526), even if it was only an assault on heaven.

On 18 March, the revolutionary Parisian people understood the betrayal of the bourgeoisie and affirmed themselves as "the self-sacrificing champion of France" (M-E, XXII, 547) that had to be regenerated by destroying the political and social conditions that had engendered the Second Empire and had matured to the point of decay. But for this, the revolutionary proletariat aimed further than the Republic, which was only a stage. The 18th of March revealed the true meaning of the Republic; the Parisian people made their defense reflex the first act of a social revolution, a *communist revolution*.

Part II
THE PARIS COMMUNE 1871

26 March to Sunday 28 May 1871

"Yes, gentlemen, the Commune intended to abolish that class-property which makes the labour of the many the wealth of the few. It aimed at the expropriation of the expropriators. It wanted to make individual property a truth by transforming the means of production, land and capital, now chiefly the means of enslaving and exploiting labour, into mere instruments of free and associated labour.—But this is Communism, "impossible" Communism!!" (M-E, XXII, 335)

"Compare these Parisians, storming the heavens, with the slaves to heaven of the German-Prussian Holy Roman Empire, with its posthumous masquerades reeking of the barracks, the Church, the cabbage Junkers and above all, of the philistines." (Marx to Kugelman, 12 April 1871, XLIV, 132)

"Because we are standing on the shoulders of the Paris Commune and the many years of development of German Social-Democracy, we have conditions that enable us to see clearly what we are doing in creating Soviet power." (Lenin, XXVII, 133)

"The Paris Commune of 1871 was the first, as yet weak, historic attempt of the working class to impose its supremacy." (Trotsky, *Terrorism and Communism*, 1919)

1. THE ORGANIZATION OF THE COMMUNE

"The Commune—the positive form of the Revolution against the Empire and the conditions of its existence—first essayed in the cities of Southern France, again and again proclaimed in the spasmodic movements during the siege of Paris...was at last victoriously installed on the 26th March, but it had not suddenly sprung into life on that day. It was the unchangeable goal of the work-men's revolution." (M-E, XXII, 482).

a. The results of the 26 March elections: a cacophony of trends

There were 229,000 voters out of 485,000 registered. This difference can be explained by the decrease in the Parisian population as a result of the war, the siege, the departures to the provinces and Versailles. Voter turnout was higher in the working-class districts than in the bourgeois districts. The suburbs voted by open ballot. Since all strata of the population could vote, many opponents of the CC were elected and only 13 CC members were chosen. The votes had thus turned away from these "unknown" people who were in such a hurry to leave, but the new assembly included a majority of revolutionaries from the CC, the Red Clubs, the workers' societies, the International, the republican parties linked to Jacobinism, etc.

On March 28th, during a ceremony in the Town Hall Square, the CC of the Federated National Guard proclaimed the Commune and handed over its powers. The Commune moved to the Château d'eau. 92 municipal councilors were thus elected by universal suffrage in the various districts of Paris (the 11th and 18th districts elected 7 each, and the 16th elected 2) for a population that was normally 1,873,713 inhabitants.

Social composition of the Commune

Apart from the bourgeois members of the party of the Order who will soon resign, there is a very wide variety of social conditions and also of opinions. There were many petty-bourgeois (accounting employees, doctors, teachers, lawyers, many publicists) and workers who would number 25 (E. Varlin, the bookbinder, the clerk Benoît Malon, the carpenter Pindy, the launderer Grêlier, the hatter Amouroux, the chaser Theiz, the foundryman Duval, the mechanic Assi, the turner Langevin, etc.). These workers were more craftsmen than workers in large-scale industry, and half of them belonged to the International.

Political trends

22 members of the Commune did not want to sit and resigned; they were replaced in the supplementary elections of 16 April (very few Parisians moved; the following were elected: the adventurer Cluseret, the worker Eugène Pottier, the worker member of the International Serraillier, E. Dupont, member of the

General Council of the International in London, the painter Gustave Courbet, Charles Longuet, future son-in-law of Marx, Garibaldi, Viard, etc.).

The three main political groups are the internationalists, the Blanquists and the Jacobins.

There are more than fifteen Internationalists: the tireless E. Varlin, the Proudhonian B. Malon, the Hungarian worker Léo Frankel, who had founded a German section of the IWMA in Paris and who knew Marx and his theories, of which he would be one of the representatives within the Commune, the Proudhonian worker Thiez, the worker Dupont, Pindy, the mechanic Assi who had already organized the strikes at Le Creusot in 1870, of which he was one of the representatives within the Commune, Langevin, Avrial, the jewellers Combault and Camelinat, Serraillier, the journalist Charles Longuet from Provence, the Blanquist trade employee Cournet who joined the IWMA in 1871, the Blanquist Edouard Vaillant; the Blanquist worker Duval, already a member of the CC like Varlin; Babick. These members of the International, with the exception of a few Blanquists, were attached to the doctrines of Proudhon: mutualism and the autonomy of communes. They opposed the use of the phraseology and methods of 1793 (committee of public salvation) and were moderates.

The Blanquists were mainly represented by Eudes, Duval (a member of the IWMA), Ranvier, Ferré, Rigault, men of unquestionable revolutionary courage, energy and fanaticism. They had the cult of 1793, and, trained in discipline according to the principles of the old coal mines, they needed their leader, who would be lacking (Blanqui was arrested on 17 March 1871, when he was ill and resting far from Paris).

The Jacobins made up the majority of the Commune. They were less active than the Blanquists, and like them were attached to the traditions of 1793. They dreamed of a political revolution that would bring the democratic regime to perfection. This group was dominated by the 60-year-old republican, Charles Delescluze, who fought on the days of 1830 and 1848 and imposed it on all revolutionaries. There was also the conceited rhetorician, the "evil genius of the Commune", Felix Pyat; he worked to divide, stirring up the most violent polemics, sharpening the most sordid personal rivalries; he attacked members of the International—in this connection Marx wrote a letter to the internationalists to help them respond to Pyat's attacks.

This division is in fact very schematic, as there were other characters that are difficult to fit into one of the blocks. The 72-year-old Proudhonian and Fourierist Beslay, who was entrusted with the presidency of the first session of the Commune, was head of industry and one of the founders of the IWMA, from which he soon left; he was too conciliatory in his dealings with the Banque de France. Gustave Flourens, a scientist with a blanquist tendency who had met Marx in 1870, and Don Quixote, who had already made wild attempts during the Empire, died on 3 April. The Blanquist millionaire Tridon, who was in favor of the ideas of the International. The Proudhonian journalist Vermorel, who had been in contact with Engels and was slandered during the Commune by Pyat; he died voluntarily on a barricade. There was also the great painter Gustave Courbet, the accountant Jourde, a Proudhonian who later became a member of the French Workers' Party, the former blanquist officer Brunel, the writer Jules Vallès, the author of the song "Le temps des cerises" Jean Baptiste Clément.

Conflict between majority and minority

This separation between two clear-cut parties took place from 28th April, during the discussion on whether or not to set up a Committee of Public Safety. 22 members of the Commune, including internationalists joined by Tridon, Vallès, Courbet, Vermorel and Jourde, among others, formed this minority, which according to Lissagaray included the most intelligent and enlightened members of the Commune, but opposed to the creation of the Committee of Public Safety. It was a tiresome quarrel between the majority and the minority which became exasperating. The minority even announced its withdrawal from the Commune by publishing a manifesto in the newspapers, to the great joy of the people of Versailles who were rejoicing at the quarrels. It will resume on May 17, but too late.

b. The Commune, legislative and executive bodies

From 29 March, the Commune decided to form commissions corresponding to the various ministries that the CC had taken over, with the exception of that of worship, which was abolished.

At Finance, there is Varlin—who, tirelessly, will move from Finance to Subsistence, then to the Revenue Office—and Jourde, a right-wing Proudhonian and a man of integrity. The latter endeavored to collect traditional revenues and avoid waste. The intermediary between the Banque de France and the Commune was the Proudhonian Beslay, who was far too moderate. Bourgin wrote: "For nine weeks of government and maintaining an army of 170,000 men on average, the CC and the Commune spent a little over 46,300,000 francs, of which 16,696,000 were provided by the Bank, the rest by the services that were

put back on their feet, in particular the grant which brought in 12 million"…
while Thiers drew on the Bank of France for 257,630,000 francs in drafts!!

At the Subsistance, Viard had to take rapid action because Paris had suffered from hunger during the siege. He taxed bread and meat, and, in liaison with the town halls, he ensured the control of the halls and markets.

The Sûreté Générale was entrusted to the Blanquist Rigault, who, with his friends, made a turbulent mess, and by his "raids of cassocks" exasperated the Catholics. This 24-year-old student took Da Costa, who was only 20 years old, as his chief of staff.

The Post Office Hotel was entrusted to the chiseler Theiz, who found it in great disarray. He regularly ran the post office service in Paris and "managed" for the province.

Camélinat, a bronze fitter, operated the Mint; Alavoine, the National Printing Office; Avrial, the Armament Material Directorate; Combault and Faillet, the direct and indirect contributions department. At the Justice Department, the Blanquist lawyer Protot decided that recourse to the judge should be free of charge, that their elections should be free of charge and that the venality of judicial officers should be abolished: the aim of these measures was to remove the class character of the exercise of justice.

The delegate for public education was Edouard Vaillant, who succeeded in reorganizing the primary schools deserted by the religious. He promoted free and secular schooling, tried to promote girls' education and vocational training. Courbet was appointed president of the Federation of Artists.

At the Labor, Industry and Exchange Commission, Léo Frankel was assisted by an initiative commission composed of workers; with him also worked B. Malon, Theiz, Dupont and Avrial. They took social measures concerning the Mount of Piety, rents and night work.

The External Relations Commission, chaired by the moderate J.B Paschal-Grousset, journalist and writer, had only an insignificant role, and did nothing to liaise with foreign countries. The delegate sent only a few emissaries to the provinces. Proclamations were sent by balloon to the departments, including that of the journalist Léo André, who addressed the peasants as follows: "Brother, you are being deceived. Our interests are the same".

The War Delegation was initially entrusted to the delegate Eudes, to the military commander of the Paris Prefecture Duval and to the commander of the Place, Bergeret. Then the Commune added the adventurous general Cluseret to Eudes.

The administrative machinery of Paris thus functioned with 10,000 employees instead of the previous 60,000. The Commune was thus both a legislative and an executive body. The executive power was entrusted to an Executive Commission which was to give the impetus to this system; it included: Eudes, Tridon, Vaillant, Duval, Pyat, Bergeret. However, on the first of May, as the military situation worsened, it was decided to create a Committee of Public Safety, despite the opposition of the minority.

c. Its program: a Universal Republic!

On 19 April, in a declaration, the Commune explained its aims to the French people. It spoke of the recognition and consolidation of the Republic, a republic that was not centralised, but which would be the result of the federation of all the communes of France. The rights of the Commune were then enumerated: voting of the communal budget, organization of the magistracy, the police, education, recruitment of all civil servants by election or competition (they would therefore be revocable), administration of the property belonging to the Commune, absolute guarantee of individual freedom, freedom of trade, freedom of work; permanent intervention of the citizens in the affairs of the Commune, organization of the National Guard through the election of chiefs. The Commune refuses the "despotic, unintelligent, arbitrary or onerous" centralization that was imposed on France by the monarchy, the Empire and the parliamentary republic. "We have the mission to accomplish the modern revolution, the largest and most fertile of all those that have illuminated history."

Obviously, the Commune sought to make this program known to the rest of France, but it did not have much time to do so. Parisians affirmed the brotherhood of peoples, conceived the whole world united in republican form: "Long live the Universal Republic!" was acclaimed during the Commune and written at the bottom of the proclamations.

The Parisian revolution received the support of many foreigners. Two thousand of them swelled the ranks of the Communards: mostly Belgians (the Belgian Federal Legion held important posts in the Communard army), Luxembourgers, Italians (Almicare Cipriani, Giuseppe Garibaldi), Poles (the generals of the Commune, Dombrovski and Wroblevski of exceptional bravery) who were numerous in Paris after the failure of the national uprising of 1863 against the Tsarism, Hungarians (Leo Frankel) but also some Swiss, Russians (Elisabeth Dmitrieff, Marx's correspondent), etc.... whom the Commune considered to be "soldiers of the Universal Republic".

In *The Civil War...* (M-E, XXII, 338) Marx writes: "...the Commune annexed to France the working people all over the world... The Commune admitted all foreigners to the honour of dying for an immortal cause... The Commune made a German working-mana its Minister of Labour... The Commune honoured the heroic sons of Poland by placing them at the head of the defenders of Paris".

d. The insurgents

It is not only these men of the Commune who are in power, but the people of Paris as a whole through the sections of the IWMA, the trade union chambers that are coming back to life, the cooperatives, the vigilance committees of the districts headed by the CC of the 20 arrondissements, the clubs.

Participation of women and children

Indeed, women participated in this revolution. Louise Michel took part in Montmartre on 18 March and with her, many other women and children. Jules Vallès, in *Le Vengeur* of April 12, 1871, enthusiastically describes: "I saw three revolutions, and for the first time I saw women, women and children, resolutely taking part in them. It seems that this revolution is precisely theirs and that by defending it they are defending their own future".

The first mass women's movement was then created with the "Union of Women for the Defense of Paris and the Relief of the Wounded" founded by the 20-year-old Russian, Elisabeth Dmitrieff, Marx's correspondent, and Nathalie Lemel, a 45-year-old bookbinder from Brittany; the journalist Léo André and many others... Proudhonism, which many members of the Commune claimed to be, was nevertheless a supported of the housewife.

The Commune proposed public education for women, with equal pay for equal work. They took part in community management and self-managed workshops. The Commune officialized free union, giving the family constituted outside marriage its first legal recognition. Finally, the Commune banned prostitution considered "as the commercial exploitation of human creatures by other human creatures".

The women manifested themselves in the Vigilance Committees of women citizens, the clubs, and Louise Michel demanded the right of women to defend the revolution with arms in hand. The Journal *Officiel* of 13 April 1871 published a citizens' address to the Executive Commission of the Paris Commune in which women demanded the right to fight and die in defense of the Commune, the possibility of obtaining rooms in town halls to meet, and money to print notices. They were so active that the English newspaper *The Times* exclaimed: "If the French nation were composed only of women, what a terrible nation it would be!"

Many women workers had been forced by the appalling misery that followed the Franco-Prussian war and the siege of Paris to prostitute themselves in order to survive. But during the Commune, they became canteen attendants, ambulance drivers, barricadiers, soldiers on the ramparts, hospital employees, or they hunted down those who refused.

During the bloody week, the women fought fiercely.

Arthur Rimbaud, who in May 1871 wrote other desperate hymns to the Paris Commune, glorified them with his Jeanne-Marie, and JB Clément dedicated the "Time of Cherries" to Louise, the nurse at the Fontaine-au-roi (rue du 10ème arrondissement) who was at his side to defend the barricade. The devotion of the children and adolescents was equally extraordinary. They joyfully gave their lives on the barricades and in front of the firing squads; the testimonies of their heroism are numerous.

Among the Versaillais, the communards aroused hatred: they were described as *petrollers* (arsonists), and Alexandre Dumas fils, author of the infamous drama *La dame aux Camélias*, dared to write: "We will say nothing about their females out of respect for all the women they resemble when they are dead"!

Social composition of the insurgents

The statistics of the individuals arrested, made by the military justice system, give an idea of the insurgents of 1871, and confirm, if need be, that the insurgents were mainly workers.

Thus, among the decrees of the government of Thiers during and after the bloody week are the following:

8% employed; 8% small traders, small renters, professionals; 5% domestic servants.

15% day laborers; 16% rough construction workers; 12% more skilled metal workers. This is the mass of the insurgents.

Finally, craftsmen of the old Parisian trades (8% of furniture, 8% of clothing, 10% of art works), many of whom were executives, officers and non-commissioned officers of the Commune.

2. THE HISTORY OF THE COMMUNE

26 March-28 May 1871

"When the Paris Commune took the management of the revolution in its own hands; when plain working men for the first time dared to infringe upon the Governmental privilege of their 'natural superiors'... the old world writhed in convulsions of rage at the sight of the Red Flag, the symbol of the Republic of Labour, floating over the Hôtel de Ville." (M-E, XXII, 336)

a. The rebellion of the slavers

The first attempt of the slave traders' conspiracy to kill Paris was to have the Prussians occupy the city; but it failed when Bismarck refused to intervene, waiting for a better time. The second, on 18 March, led to the rout of the army and the flight of the government and administration to Versailles.

In Versailles, the bourgeoisie, with its puppet Thiers, methodically prepared its next attack. It was necessary to find an army, cut Paris off from the provinces and, to save time, simulate negotiations.

The army of counter-revolution

The remnants of the line regiments were small in numbers and unsafe. Thiers' urgent appeals to the provinces were met with outright refusal. The Vendée alone provided a handful of royalists who fought under a white flag to the cries of: Long live Jesus, long live the King! Thiers was therefore forced to hastily assemble a colorful band of sailors, marines, pontifical zouaves, Valentin's gendarmes, city sergeants and Pietri's spies. But this army would have been ridiculously impotent without the repatriation of imperial prisoners of war that Bismarck was releasing bit by bit, just enough to stir up civil war and keep the government of Versailles under Prussia. This painfully united army remained so reliable for Thiers that it was watched over by the Versailles police!

Cutting Paris off from the province

"While the Versailles Government, as soon as it had recovered some spirit and strength, used the most violent means against the Commune; while it put down the free expression of opinion all over France, even to the forbidding of meetings of delegates from the large towns; while it subjected Versailles and the rest of France to an espionage far surpassing that of the Second Empire; while it burned by its gendarme inquisitors all papers printed at Paris, and sifted all correspondence from and to Paris; while in the National Assembly the most timid attempts to put in a word for Paris were howled down... with the savage warfare of Versailles outside, and its attempts at corruption and conspiracy inside Paris." (M-E, XXII, 340)

The Commune was keen to observe all the conventions and appearances of liberalism, as if in peace. For Thiers had clearly understood that it was fundamental that Paris be cut off from the province (on 13 May, delegates of the Republican Union League who were on their way to Bordeaux were arrested; a meeting of delegates in Lyon was forbidden...). Communes broke up intermittently in the various large cities of France; only Paris would have been able to link them together, to lead the revolution on a national scale.

The comedy of conciliation

Deputations and addresses were pouring in from everywhere on Thiers, demanding reconciliation with Paris: the mayors and deputies of Paris on 25 March, the freemasons on 10 April, the delegates of the trade union chambers on 11. Brunet, deputy for the Seine, on 20 April proposed the appointment of a pacification commission, a proposal which was met with an explosion of hatred from the rural population; the Republican Union League of Trade and Industry Delegates on 6 May, and other provincial delegations tried to intervene... So much so that Dufaure, Minister of Justice of Thiers, asked the prosecutors on 23 April to treat "the word conciliation as a crime"!

In fact, Thiers was concerned from the outset to accompany his war of bandits against Paris with a little conciliatory comedy that was to serve more than one purpose. First to deceive the province, then to deceive the bourgeois elements of the Commune and thus gain time; finally to give the avowed republicans of the National Assembly the opportunity to hide their betrayal of Paris.

Thus on 21 March, as he had no army at the time, he declared to the National Assembly that he would never attack Paris; on the 27th, that he was determined to maintain the Republic, but that he would bring down the communal revolution in Lyon and Marseille in the name of this same Republic, even though the bawling of the rural representatives covered the simple mention of this name and his Dufaure was acting behind the scenes.

Dufaure, this old Orléanist lawyer, already there in 1839 under Louis Philippe, in 1849 under Louis Bonaparte, had the National Assembly pass a series of repressive laws which, after the fall of Paris, were to eradicate the last vestiges of republican freedom, repealed the procedure of courts martial and introduced a draconian deportation law (the 1848 revolution had abolished the death penalty which was then replaced by deportation).

Finally, Thiers decided to organize nationwide municipal elections for 30 April, hoping, thanks to the intrigues of his prefects and police intimidation that the verdict of the provinces would give the Assembly the moral and material power it needed to conquer Paris. On this occasion, on 17 April, he played one of his great scenes of conciliation, presenting himself as the defender of the Republic under attack by a "handful" of Parisian conspirators, a handful that had to be punished, the only ones to be punished! But the ruminant-brained brains of his country folk understood nothing of his game and welcomed his sentimental speech with further bellowing of rage.

The municipal elections of 30 April

France turned a deaf ear to the siren song of Thiers! Of the 700,000 town councillors elected by the remaining 35,000 municipalities, the legitimists, Orléans and Bonapartists did not count 8,000. To complete the collapse, the newly elected town councilors of the cities of France openly threatened the usurping Assembly of Versailles with a counter-assembly in Bordeaux.

Thiers and its rural supporters were therefore in a very bad position. But Bismarck was only waiting for a bad moment of this kind to impose draconian peace conditions and liquidate the Paris revolution without too much damage to Prussia.

Bismarck manoeuvres the cowardly French bourgeoisie

Bismarck summoned Thiers to send plenipotentiaries to Frankfurt for the final peace settlement. Thiers obeyed the master's call by sending his faithful Jules Favre and his finance minister Pouyer-Quertier. Pouyer-Quertier, a Rouen spinner who considered the cession of the French provinces as a means of increasing the price of his goods in France, was the perfect man for the job.

Bismarck's demands—to which both envoys hastened to comply—included a shortening of the deadlines for the payment of war indemnity, and the continued occupation of the Paris forts by Prussian troops until Bismarck was satisfied with the state of affairs in France. Prussia was thus recognized as the supreme arbiter of France's internal affairs. In return, he offered to free the imprisoned Bonapartist army for the extermination of Paris, to give direct assistance by the troops of Emperor Wilhelm and to demand payment of the first installment of the indemnity only after the "pacification" of Paris.

The peace treaty was signed on 10 May and the Versailles Assembly quickly ratified it on the 18th. With a sigh of relief and gratitude to its savior, *the French counter-revolution kissed the feet of the German counter-revolution.*

b. War on the revolution!

Just as the bourgeois government forced the CC to take on a governmental role by abandoning Paris to it, just as attacking the capital first, it forced the Commune to take the bellicose route. The military power of the Commune was divided between three people: the war delegate Eudes, to whom the Commune added the adventurer Cluseret, the military commander of the Duval police headquarters, and the stronghold commander Bergeret.

Fighting resumes in April

After the failure of 18 March, the party of the Order led by Thiers, who with Bismarck's help had reconstituted his army (more than 60,000 men), undertook regular operations against Paris. On 21 March, Vinoy had retaken the Mont Valérien fort which, in panic, Thiers had abandoned.

On April 2nd, the Versaillais attacked the federates led by Bergeret during a reconnaissance in the direction of Courbevoie. Too few in number, fearing they would be cut off from Paris, the federates evacuated Courbevoie and were driven back to the Neuilly bridge. The gendarmes of Versailles took five prisoners and shot them at the foot of Mont Valérien. When the news came out and the "siege begins again" ran through Paris, the same explosion came from all the districts and 50,000 men gathered in a single cry: To Versailles! The Commune had to react. The executive commission met and issued a proclamation: "The royalist conspirators have attacked!... Our duty is to defend the great city against these shameful aggressions". In fact, there was a lively discussion within the commission. Duval, Bergeret and Eudes were vigorously in favor of the attack; Tridon, Vaillant, Lefrançais, F.Pyat (who had been shouting for three days: "To Versailles!") resisted, adding Cluseret to Eudes, believing they were putting a serious soldier at war. This lack of cohesion explains in large part the failure of the sortie of 3 April: no serious plan, no coordination established between the various officers and between them and the Commune, no determination to fight the enemy energetically. The four civilian members asked the generals to present a detailed account of their forces in terms of men, artillery, ammunition and transport. But the generals left without formal orders, tired of this procrastination.

The April 3rd sortie

Marx wrote about it (*The Civil War...*): "The march on Versailles was decided, prepared and undertaken by the CC without the knowledge of the Commune and even in opposition to its clearly expressed will".

The exit plan was based on the certainty of the neutrality of Mont Valérien and on the illusion of a "promenade" through Versailles on three columns which were to meet at a certain point: one on the right, commanded by Bergeret assisted by Flourens with 15,000 men, concentrated at Rueil to attack Versailles from the north, one in the center, commanded by Eudes with 10,000 men and one on the left, commanded by Duval with 3,000 men. The generals sent orders to the legion chiefs to form columns on the right and left banks. But these movements without experienced staff officers were executed very badly. Many battalions had been without leaders since 18 March, the national guards without cadres and the improvised generals without experience. They neglected the most elementary provisions, did not gather artillery or ambulances, forgot to draw up an agenda and left the men without food for several hours. Each federated took the leader it wanted. Many did not have cartridges, believing according to the newspapers that they were simply going for a military walk, as Lissagaray recounts. Each of these armies was an adventurous rabble, devoid of everything. Of the 100,000 that had been talked about at the beginning, only 23,000 were mobilized!

For the right-hand column, the disorder began as soon as the first cannonades of Mont Valérien, which it was thought would not fire, began to rain; while Bergeret was forced to withdraw towards Paris, the bold Flourens continued his march on Rueil, finding a heroic death there on the arrival of reinforcements sent by Vinoy. Another defeat struck the left column, unable to respond to enemy fire and therefore forced to retreat to Chatillon; Duval died there at the cry of "Vive la Commune" against the firing squad of the Versaillais. Finally, the central column had to withdraw to Fort Issy because it was unable to respond to the enemy artillery.

During this time, the Commune held a session from 10 o'clock in the evening until midnight, but nobody mentioned the sortie to Versailles!

Instead of learning from this drama, blaming the perpetrators of the mistakes, it left them free to conduct military operations. Their carelessness and incapacity had been fatal, but "the Commune understood that it was responsible and that, to be fair, it should have blamed itself as well" (Lissagaray).

Cluseret the adventurer

After this disaster, the ardor of the masses was cooled. The Commune lost all hesitation and the Parisian defense gave up the offensive for good, confining itself to purely defensive tactics. Cluseret thus became the master of the Commune's military destiny.

This officer trained at Saint Cyr, the son of an officer, former officer of the mobile guard who in June 1848 had crushed the rebellious workers under the orders of Cavaignac, who enlisted in Italy under Garibaldi, then in America, in Ireland, had become a "professional" insurgent general. He joined the IWMA in 1868 and, in Lyon, on 28 September 1870, the rioters called him; he came with Bakunin, was acclaimed, but did nothing and disappeared. He made an appearance in Marseilles where he became head of the brief Commune of Marseilles in November 1870. On 30 March he was appointed head of the National Guard and on 3 April the Commune delegated him to the War; but he was careful not to prevent the 3 April exit, which would discredit his rivals.

He used the art of bluffing: he announced the reorganization of the federated army to the press, but did nothing. He was only there to enrich his career with a new adventure. As soon as he arrived at the ministry, he tried to eliminate a whole part of the National Guard by forming a "sedentary National Guard" for married National Guards.

He did not attempt any serious offensive against Versailles. Apart from a few helpings due to the initiative of leaders like Dombrowski, the defense of Paris appeared to be totally passive.

The Commune gets bogged down

The Commune did not learn any lessons from the 3 April outing, apart from a decree on hostages, in response to the executions of the Versailles people, which was not applied. The fighting only got worse and worse. On 7 April, the Versaillais seized the passage from the Seine to Neuilly on the western front of Paris. The bombardments of this part of Paris did not stop, so that on the 25th a suspension of arms was accepted by Versailles to allow the inhabitants of Neuilly (these were not the proletarian districts) to evacuate their locality. On 8 April, Mac Mahon was appointed head of the Versailles army. On 26 April, De Cissey and the Versailles troops occupied the Moulineaux; on the 27th, it was the massacre of 4 federates taken prisoner by the Versailles people at La Belle-Epine near Villejuif. On 28–29, Versailles operations took place against Fort Issy in the hands of the federates, after it had been abandoned for a while.

The Executive Commission set up on 20 April does not manage to improve the internal and above all military situation vis-à-vis the Versailles people. On 28 April, Jules Miot, a member of the Commune, proposed to the Commune Council the creation of a Committee of Public Safety (imitating what the Montagnards of 1793 had done to face the many dangers threatening the Republic). This proposal met with the opposition of a minority of the elected representatives of the Commune, including internationalists and others. In fact, the federal council of the Parisian sections of the IWMA saw in this committee a dictatorial power which would be in formal opposition to the democratic political aspirations of the Commune's electorate! It was only on 1 May that the Committee was accepted by 45 votes to 23.

A committee of 5 members was elected: Gabriel Ranvier, the only one with real energy, Léo Meillet, Armand Arnaud, Charles Gérardin, Félix Pyat (who resigned on 5 May); but it was no better than the Executive Commission. On 8 May a new committee was elected with Blanquists or Jacobins: Charles Delescluze (who would be replaced by Edouard Billioray on 10 May), Emiles Eudes, Charles Gambon,

On 1 May, the Commune dismissed Cluseret, who had abandoned the Issy fort left without troops (he fled on 24 May), and replaced him with the generous colonel Louis Rossel, a career soldier, who tried in vain to reorganize the army of the federated powers. This soldier, a polytechnicien, had joined the Commune for patriotic reasons. He tried to delimit the responsibilities of military leaders such as Dombrowski, La Cécilia, Wrobleswski, Bergeret and Eudes. But he was to neglect the internal defense of Paris, and faced with the claims of the CC, he preferred to resign (he will be shot on 28 November).

The Public Salvation Committee interfered with the decisions of the war delegate, Louis Rossel. It let the CC get into the war services. In fact, from 30 March, the CC of the National Guard regained its strength and arrogated to itself a singular authority with regard to the guard; on 1 April, it claimed the Intendancy, the right to appoint the chief of staff and since then it did not cease to claim the administration of the war for which it set up special commissions. The minority of the Commune demanded its dissolution, but it had the support of the majority and of the Committee of Public Safety.

c. The victory of the counter-revolution

Bismarck's help

Paris never had more than 40,000 combatants, to which must be added women and adolescents.

Thiers, on the contrary, with the support of Bismarck, had strengthened its army: it numbered 65,000 combatants to which were added 135,000 prisoners gradually released from Germany. This numerical advantage gave the Versaillais a decisive superiority from the beginning of May. This became apparent on 23rd April when Thiers broke off the negotiations begun by the Commune and aimed at exchanging hostages for the only Blanqui! His language, so cautious until then, became threatening and brutal, and as soon as Mac Mahon assured him that he could soon enter Paris, Thiers no longer spoke to the Assembly of conciliation but of complete expiation.

The encirclement of Paris

From the first days of May, Paris was bombarded by the Versaillais and the fight against the raging Versailles troops absorbed all the energies of the Commune.

On the southern front, the Versaillais took by treason the Moulin-Saquet redoubt (at Vitry sur Seine, west of Paris) on 3–4 May; on the 9th, the besieged Fort d'Issy was destroyed by cannon fire and occupied by the Versaillais. In a letter to Jung dated 10 May, Engels considered that "Those fellows that ran away from Fort Issy without being attacked deserve to be shot. The military situation has become much worse through this piece of cowardice".(M-E, XLIV, 148)

Weary, Rossel resigned and was replaced by the old Jacobin Delescluze. This civilian delegate knew little about military matters. Dombrowski, a former officer in the Russian army, an insurgent in Poland, was his best collaborator.

The situation of the federated army was more than confused. Paris was swarming with general staffs since there were no heads: the war delegation, the Place, the generals, each legion had a general staff. The Intendancy was often a veritable chaos. So much so that while the Versailles army was growing stronger, the federated army melted away, and the lack of organization meant that the dedicated battalions remained in line indefinitely. Thus the army of the Commune only had between 10,000 and 15,000 men left to fight against the Versailles army, which numbered more than 100,000. But there were 120,000 National Guards in Paris who received their pay.

On 13 May, the fort of Vanves fell.

d. The bloody week: from Sunday 21st May to Sunday 28th May.

Mac Mahon's Versailles army, reinforced after the return of the prisoners freed by Bismarck, entered Paris without firing a shot or receiving a single shell on Sunday 21 May through the Porte de Saint Cloud left defenseless by the federates, when treason had opened the gates of Paris to General Douayl! The Prussians who occupied the forts in the north and east allowed the Versaillais to advance on the ground north of Paris, which was forbidden to them by the armistice, thus allowing them to attack on a wide front which the Parisians believed to be protected by the convention, and where they therefore had only a small number of troops. Thus there was little resistance in the western half of Paris, the city of luxury itself. On the other hand, it became more violent as the Versaillais approached the working-class neighborhood of the eastern half of Paris.

Thiers, seeing his army ready on one side and the Prussians closing their eyes on the other, gave carte blanche to the cries of: "I shall be pitiless! The expiation will be complete, and justice will be stern!" The bloodthirsty soldiers rushed to revolutionary Paris to perpetrate an abominable carnage. The cause of bourgeois justice, order and civilization was to triumph! Mac Mahon with his henchman, General Galiffet, began a methodical reconquest of Paris, by firing guns, cannons and setting fires. During their advance, the Versailles people shot all those they found with arms in their hands.

The Commune struggles desperately

On the evening of 21 May, when the Commune learned of the Versaillais entrance, it raised the session, resting on the Committee of Public Safety, which was content to cover the walls with proclamations and suddenly stopped existing. Like the Commune, the delegate for War, Delescluze, renounced the action at the decisive moment. On the morning of the 22nd, he abdicated his military authority and posted: "Enough militarism... Make way for the people, for the bare-armed combatants". As Lissagaray wrote: "Instead of 200 strategic barricades that were easy to defend, hundreds were created that were impossible to man"! The war of the barricades, the one that all wage in their own neighborhood: a desperate struggle set Paris on fire. With the communal army dispersing itself in this way in the districts, without a centralized command. The CC tried to intervene, but to no avail: the struggle continued at random, blow by blow, in the face of the Versailles war machine which deliberately progressed slowly in order to mercilessly crush revolutionary Paris in strenuous fighting that was exhausting for the insurgents.

The heroism of revolutionary Paris

Revolutionary Paris launched itself into battle with the energy of despair, the generosity of those who do not surrender.

Paris defended its revolution street by street, barricade by barricade until it succumbed. It used fire—to the great scandal of the bourgeois gentlemen who, for their part, set Paris ablaze with their shells; not to mention the Bonapartist agents who lit fires to remove the traces of imperial management—mainly to defend themselves and slow the enemy's advance. Ah, those "petrol women" who set fire to Paris to forbid the troops of Versailles to enter the long avenues opened expressly by Hausmann for the fire of the bourgeois artillery, how much hatred they provoked in the bourgeoisie! The Tuileries, the Conseil d'État, the Cour des Comptes, the Ministry of Finance, the Louvre Library, the Town Hall burned. The Communards also set fire to the police headquarters and the courthouse in the center of Paris, while sparing Notre Dame and the Sainte Chapelle.

Hallali

On the 21st, the Versaillais occupied the Trocadéro, the gates of Sèvres and of Versailles, the 15th arrondissement. On the 22nd, Douay and his troops were on the Champs Elysées, de Cissey occupied the Montparnasse station; General Ladmirault reached the outer boulevards up to the gates of Asnières and Clichy and later took the gates of Saint Ouen and Montmartre. Barricades were erected at Batignolles, rue de Rivoli, at the crossroads of Chateaudun and in the 9th arrondissement.

On the 23rd, the Batignolles were taken and the nearby Montmartre hills were surrounded by the Versaillais who were advancing towards the center and burning the quays with their shells.

On the 24th, the Commune moved to the 11th Town Hall. The Versaillais thus reached the Bank of France and the Louvre, and massacred the federates there found.

On the 25th, the barricades were still defended in the 2nd and 3rd arrondissements, as were the Butte-aux-Cailles and the Château d'Eau. The last session of the Commune took place on the same day at the Town Hall of the 20th arrondissement, then located at 136 rue de Paris (rue de Belleville). Ranvier, Trinquet, Ferré, Varlin, Vallès, Vaillant and Jourde took part. Delescluze was killed on the barricades of the Place du Château d'Eau (Place de la République).

On the 26th, the Commune had only three or four thousand fighters left to face Mac Mahon's five army corps. The Prussians had facilitated the encirclement movement by the north of Paris and formed an impassable cordon from the Marne to Montreuil (the Saxon army corps let the hunted communards pass the following days). The Versaillais took Ménilmontant and Belleville. And on the 27th, an island of resistance was maintained in the 20th arrondissement, but the attack of the Versaillais against the Père Lachaise cemetery resulted in 1600 killed or shot in the middle of the tombs; other mass executions with machine guns followed until the beginning of June.

Insurgents including Ferré tried to respond to this violence by shooting about sixty hostages on 26 May at 85 rue Haxo (34 gendarmes, 10 religious including Archbishop Darboy, snitches were shot against the wall at 53 rue Borrego) that Varlin, Vallès and Serrailier tried to save all the same.

On May 28th, the last barricades in Belleville, rue du Faubourg du Temple and rue Ramponneau, fell. Varlin was recognized there, lynched and shot. Vermorel, Delescluze, Dombrowski, Rigault, Vermorel, Lillière and many others were killed.

On the 29th, the fort of Vincennes capitulated and its nine officers were shot on the spot.

The communards had fought with a rage of despair, causing havoc in the Versailles ranks: 5 generals killed and 10 wounded, 78 officers killed and 420 wounded, 794 soldiers killed and more than 6,000 wounded. The revenge was terrible.

A carnage

> To find a parallel for the conduct of Thiers and. his blood-hounds we must go back to the times of Sulla and the two Triumvirates of Rome. The same wholesale slaughter in cold blood; the same disregard, in massacre, of age and sex; the same system of torturing prisoners; the same proscriptions, but this time of a whole class; the same savage hunt after concealed leaders, lest one might escape; the same denunciations of political and private enemies; the same indifference for the butchery of entire strangers to the feud. There is but this difference, that

the Romans had no mitrailleuses for the despatch, in the lump, of the proscribed, and that they had not "the law in their hands", nor on their lips the cry of "civilization" (M-E, XXII (348-349).

The rage of the bourgeoisie in June 1848 that killed 3,000 workers was child's play compared to the unspeakable infamy of 1871 with its butchery of tens of thousands of revolutionaries—men, women and children. General De Gallifet distinguished himself by his cruelty, which was far superior to that of a Cavaignac. On 9 June, *Paris-journal* wrote again: "It is at the Bois de Boulogne that people sentenced to death by court-martial will be executed in the future. Every time the number of condemned men exceeds ten, the firing squad will be replaced by a machine gun".

"About 30,000 Parisians were shot down by the bestial soldiery, and about 45,000 were arrested, many of whom were afterwards executed, while thousands were transported or exiled. In all, Paris lost about 100,000 of its best people, including some of the finest workers in all trades". (Lenin, XVII, 135).

Mass graves were dug in Saint Jacques square, Monceau park, Père Lachaise (where the "Wall of the federates" is located, against which hundreds of federates were shot on 28th May). From May 1871 to December 1874, there were 24 war councils for 80 children, 132 women and 9950 men from the Commune, with sentences of forced labor, deportations to the fortified enclosure at Cayenne in French Guiana or New Caledonia, and death sentences (Théophile Ferré and Louis Rossel were executed). Certain industries such as furniture and shoemaking were completely emptied of their workers: "Parisian industry," wrote Lissagaray, "was crushed".

Many of the survivors took refuge in London, where the IWMA General Council looked after them, in Belgium and Switzerland.

Of course the IWMA was persecuted throughout Europe. In France, the law of March 1872 provided for the imprisonment and fine of any Frenchman affiliated to the International. Henceforth, the French section could only live in the form of a secret society and was nothing more than a skeleton.

The amnesty of 1880 brought the survivors back to France.

Glory to the Commune, furnace of a new society!

Bismarck was satisfied; he contemplated the ruins of Paris and the corpses of the Parisian proletarians. For him it was not only a question of the extermination of the Revolution, but also of the extinction of France, now beheaded, and by the French government itself.

Marx exclaimed thus at the end of *The Civil War...*, in London on 30 May 1871: "Working men's Paris, with its Commune, will be for ever celebrated as the glorious harbinger of a new society. Its martyrs are enshrined in the great heart of the working class. Its exterminators history has already nailed to that eternal pillory from which all the prayers of their priests will not avail to redeem them" (M-E, XXII, 355).

3. THE PROVINCE

The Paris Commune was not an isolated event in the France of the Second Empire. Communist uprisings broke out in the provinces, some of which preceded the one in Paris. The revolutionary situation thus concerned all of France, but was expressed most violently in Paris, which, by taking on the role of the heart of France, centralized all the revolutionary energies and consequently all the strength of the revolutionary wave. The Paris Commune was the culmination of a dispersed insurrectional movement that lasted almost a year: its culmination and its end. The provisional government, conscious of the danger of provincial movements and of the link between them and the Paris Commune, delegated the lawyer Léon Gambetta, an ardent republican, to bring order to the provinces. The latter, a patriot, was forced to submit to the capitular will of the Trochu government, having in common with him the fear of the insurrectional movement. Minister of the Interior of the national defense government, he left Paris in a balloon on 7 October with two other ministers to organize new armies in Tours and then in Bordeaux to defend Paris, besieged by the Prussians, and to calm the unrest in the provinces. He carried out the government's order to block the communal elections in the provinces and to make all the Bonapartist personnel who were sabotaging the war and discouraging all those who flocked to "defend the Fatherland" stay at their posts. In February 1871, faced with the electoral victory of the monarchists and partisans of Thiers, he resigned but did not join the revolutionaries of the Commune. He did not return to Paris until June 1871.

Communes were thus born in the south-east, Isère, Saint Etienne, Le Creusot and Limoges, which sometimes lasted only a few days.

a. The South-East

The section of the IWMA founded in Marseille in 1867, under Bakunist influence, was very organized and active. The Bakunist, typographer André Bastelica, the main leader of the Marseilles section of the IWMA, animated it with enthusiasm. In March 1870 a resounding congress of the IWMA took place in Lyon with the participation of Varlin, Bastelica and Bakunin, who affirmed the will of the federations to intensify revolutionary action. The imperial government then had some militants arrested, including Varlin; Bastelica fled to Spain.

In the elections of 1869, the contribution of workers militants had ensured the victory of the Republican candidates. Marseilles voted "no" in the Bonapartist plebiscite of 8 May 1870; at that time Marseilles was a flourishing city of 315,000 inhabitants, the largest port in France.

After the proclamation of the Republic in Paris, a "popular" power was installed on 5 September; the ideas of the Revolutionary Commune and of federation were tested there in a situation where the requirements of national defense played a decisive role. This insurrectional Commune was formed with the support of the section of the International and the Civic Guard formed on the 4th September.

On 14 September, when the Prussians investment on Paris was announced, subscriptions for the country in danger were opened; within a few days, 10,000 volunteers formed corps francs. On 8 September, the International declared: "It is necessary to break the administrative machine and return the initiative for action to all the revolutionary communes of France, called upon to form a new organization by federating among themselves for defense". Bastelica demanded a government of the South based on the workers, mass levying and taxing the rich. At the request of the International, Bastelica joined the Paris Commune where he headed the direct and indirect tax service. He died in exile in Switzerland in 1884 at the age of 39.

The Ligue du Midi was formed with 14 departments for the purpose of national defense. Its capital was Marseille. Léon Gambetta opposed the Ligue, because he was opposed to any autonomy of the provinces and especially to any rupture with the bourgeoisie.

A revolutionary Commune was proclaimed in Marseilles on 31 October 1870: "It is to the salvation of the whole of France that southern France wants to work". It named Cluseret, who had just arrived after the failure of the Commune in Lyon, commander of the National Guard and general-in-chief. But this Commune collapsed on 3 November. On 14 November, new municipal elections allowed the victory of the moderate list: Alphonse Gent, a friend of Gambetta, a republican, succeeded in making the policy of the government of National Defense prevail.

Gambetta immediately declared the Ligue du Midi illegal and it collapsed in general discouragement. The announcement of the revolution of 18 March 1871 in Paris was the signal for a new insurrection and a Commune was proclaimed on 23 March at the instigation of Gaston Crémieux, a republican lawyer, who, unlike his friend Gambetta, did not abandon the Commune (he was shot on 30 November 1871). The bourgeoisie, by abandoning the city to the Communards, applied Thiers' tactics towards Paris. The repression, directed from Aubagne, the Versailles of Marseille, was just as ruthless there. Two infantry battalions fraternized with the insurgents. A battery of cannons bombarded the city from Notre-Dame-de-la-Garde, renamed Notre-Dame-de-la-Bombarde by the communards. The town remained under state of siege until 1876.

There were other uprisings in Narbonne, in Toulouse where Thiers sent Keratry, the former prefect of police on 4 September, to recapture the city on 27 March.

b. Isère

The fall of the Empire was well received in Grenoble, where it was decided to raise a company of irregulars made up of volunteers after the capitulation of Sedan to defend the Republic. Foreign battalions also came to offer their services. An envoy from Gambetta also tried to set up an army of the Alps from the battalions of national guards. This company of Dauphinois snipers fought in the east under the command of Giuseppe Garibaldi. The latter had been called up under the impetus of Gambetta in 1870 by the national defense committees. On 25th and 26th November 1870, with his two sons, at the head of 10,000 French riflemen of the Vosges Army, he won the victory of Dijon against the Prussians.

In most towns and villages, battalions of national guards were formed, which demanded weapons from the prefecture. Isère joined the Ligue du Midi, again with a view to organizing national defense.

In Lyon, on the 4th September, an insurrection broke out. Mikhail Bakunin, who arrived in the city on the 15th, tried to lead the movement. But his intervention and his standpoints only underlined the divergences with the partisans of Marx within the IWMA which would end in the separation of the anarchists from the International in 1872. Marx, in a letter to Beesly of 19 October 1870, attacked Bakounine and Cluseret violently (M-E, XLIV, 89):

Under the pressure of the "International" section, the Republic was proclaimed before Paris had taken that step. A revolutionary Government was at once established— La Commune — composed partly of workmen belonging to the "International", partly of Radical middle-class Republicans. The octrois were at once abolished, and rightly so... The action of Lyons was at once felt at Marseilles and Toulouse, where the "International" sections are strong. But the asses, Bakunine and Cluseret, arrived at Lyons and spoiled everything. Belonging both to the "International", they had, unfortunately, influence enough to mislead our friends. The Hotel de Ville was seized—for a short time—and most foolish decrees... on the abolition de l'état and similar nonsense were issued. You understand that the very fact of a Russian—represented by the middle class papers as an agent of Bismarck—pretending to impose himself as the leader of a Comité du Salut de la Franceb was quite sufficient to turn the balance of public opinion. As to Cluseret, he behaved both as a fool and a coward. These two men have left Lyons after their failure.

As early as 19 March, reactions of sympathy were expressed in favor of Paris. The Commune was proclaimed in Lyon on the 22nd. Garibaldi was appointed General of the National Guard. But the Commune fell apart on the 25th.

On the whole, at the end of the Empire, the working class population of Isère led important struggles to improve their living conditions, but could not support the Paris Commune. Republicans of radical tendency contributed largely to defusing the actions in favor of Paris by launching workers in petition campaigns addressed to Versailles and by condemning the more revolutionary actions.

4. MEASURES TO LEAD TO COMMUNISM!

"The great social measure of the Commune was its own working existence." (M-E, XXII, 339).

a. The measures of the Paris Commune

The Committee on Labor, Industry and Trade

Most of these measures were taken by the Labor, Industry and Exchange Commission created on 21 April by the Commune. It was headed by the Hungarian-born jeweler Leo Frankel, a member of the International. This commission was composed almost exclusively of workers and members of the IWMA; it was joined by an initiative commission made up of workers, and in liaison with the trade union chambers.

This commission had to face two emergencies: to improve the condition of the workers and to provide employment for the unemployed who had multiplied during the siege (out of 600,000 Parisian workers, just over 100,000 were working).

For the improvement of workers' conditions, the members of the commission clashed against the majority tendency of the elected representatives of the Commune, who believed that they did not have to intervene in social questions; and to those who insisted on reaching an agreement with the bosses, Frankel replied: "I have not accepted any other mandate here than that of defending the proletariat, and when a measure is just, I accept it and I execute it without consulting the bosses". The commission acted mainly on a piecemeal basis. It thus took care of the case of the workers employed in the construction of the barricades (in fact, contrary to the "spontaneous" barricades of 1848, the largest in 1871 were erected by contractors who employed earth-movers paid by the day who demanded an increase in pay). In the same way it was the bakers who approached the commission to demand the abolition of night work and of brokers But it is nevertheless remarkable that the "labor booklet", which made the worker constantly surveilled (the Second Empire had in fact re-established in 1854 the "labor booklet" instituted by Louis XV and then by Napoleon I, i.e. a recruitment booklet held by the boss and on which it was possible to follow the progress of the worker's "career". The latter was obliged to present it at the slightest request of the police force) was not suppressed by the Commune. It was not until 1890 that this was done.

In order to combat unemployment, registers were opened in each district for job offers and applications. A balance sheet of the workshops abandoned by the bosses was drawn up by the trade union chambers and these workshops were handed over, including equipment and machinery, to the workers employed there after they had organized themselves into cooperatives. About ten workshops were confiscated for the benefit of the workers. Most of them were factories working for the army. The orders of the Commune (military clothing) were given in preference to the workers' guilds.

Frankel entrusted the organization of women's work in Paris to Elisabeth Dmitrieff who founded the Women's Union; the women workers met to appoint delegates to create trade union chambers, then a federal chamber of workers.

The movement of the workers' companies, which had slowed down since July 1870, resumed its activity with 34 trade union chambers and 43 production associations.

Measures in favor of the working class: Communism versus Proudhonism!

1. Abolition of night work for bakers and suppression of the brokers, real parasites they were obliged to turn to in order to find work. The placements were allocated to the town halls.

2. Prohibition of the practice used by employers to reduce workers' wages by levying fines under multiple pretexts, "a process by which the employer combines in his own person the roles of legislator, judge and executioner, and pockets the money on top of the market" (La guerre civile...).

3. Handing over to the workers' associations, subject to compensation to the owners, of all workshops and factories that had closed.

Engels, in his introduction from 1891 to *The Civil War...* (M-E, XXVII, 188):

> By 1871, large-scale industry had already so much ceased to be an exceptional case even in Paris, the centre of artistic handicrafts, that by far the most important decree of the Commune instituted an organisation of large-scale industry and even of manufacture which was not only to be based on the association of the workers in each factory, but also to combine all these associations in one great union; in short, an organisation which, as Marx quite rightly says in *The Civil War*, must necessarily have led in the end to communism, that is to say, the direct opposite of the Proudhon doctrine.

4. Mount of Piety: the sale of deposited objects was stopped and objects worth less than 20 francs could be redeemed free of charge. The Com-

mune ordered the removal of the site, as it constituted a private exploitation of the workers.

5. The town halls were not to distinguish between so-called illegitimate women, mothers and widows of the National Guards as far as the 75 cent compensation was concerned.

6. Intellectual emancipation: reorganization of public education by removing the religious and clerical element, by appointing a commission for the organization of primary and professional education headed by Edouard Vaillant. The Commune ordered that all school work instruments be given free of charge by the teachers who received them from the town halls.

Other general measures

1. Total remission of the rent for the last three terms until April without any compensation for the owners, no eviction notice given by the owners was valid for the next three months; requisition of abandoned premises in favor of inhabitants whose flats were damaged by the bombings.

2. Maturities (payment of maturing bills of exchange): all legal action for maturity was suspended, all bills of exchange had to be repaid over three years, without this debt bearing interest. These measures thwarted the effects of the Dufaure laws on leases and bills of exchange which had led to the bankruptcy of most Parisian merchants.

3. As regards *Justice*: notaries, bailiffs, auctioneers, registrars and other judicial officers were transformed into civil servants of the Commune, receiving a fixed salary from it like other workers.

The Commune appointed the lawyer Rigault, public prosecutor, to do the most pressing work of the Civil Court of the Seine, from which the magistrates had fled, until the reorganization of the courts by universal suffrage.

9. Creation of a commission to establish free universities that are no longer parasites of the State.

10. Other measures:

- Conscription was abolished; the standing army and police, the material instruments of power of the former government, were abolished. The National Guard was proclaimed the sole armed force.

- The separation of church and State was declared with the abolition of the church budget and the transformation of all church property into national property. Priests had to live on the alms of the faithful.

- The salary of an employee of the Commune, and therefore also of its members, could not exceed 6,000 francs (i.e. a worker's salary).

- All administrative, judicial and educational posts were subject to the choice of the persons concerned by election by universal suffrage and to dismissal at any time by the persons concerned. The Commune would impeach and arrest its generals as soon as they would be suspected of neglecting their duties.

- The two guillotines were burned, and all political prisoners incarcerated as suspects under the Bonapartist regime were released after an investigation.

- The column on Place Vendôme, cast by Napoleon I with the cannons conquered after the 1809 war by the Russian and Austrian armies on the site of a statue of Louis XIV destroyed in 1792, "as a symbol of brute force and false glory, an affirmation of militarism, a negation of international law, a permanent insult from victors to the vanquished", was demolished on 16 May 1871. It was rebuilt in 1873 (the painter Gustave Courbet, who had asked for it to be demolished on 14 September 1870, was forced to reimburse part of the costs).

- The Commune validated the election of Leo Frankel, a German member of the International, who was elected as a member of the Commune's Executive as a delegate of the Trade and Labor Commission, since the Commune's flag was that of the Universal Republic.

- The Commune abolished political and professional oaths.

- The Commune decided to destroy the monument known as the "Chapel of Atonement of Louis XVI", erected in reparation for the execution of Louis XVI, because it was a permanent insult to the first revolution and a perpetual protest of the reaction against the justice of the people.

The measures of public salvation

The disarmament of the "loyalist" national guards (obeying the Versailles government) by the CC of the National Guard Federation after the reactionary demonstration in Place Vendôme on 21 March was decided.

Unfortunately, the reprisal decree of 6 April was never implemented. In response to the massacre of the Federates perpetrated by the Versailles people, the Commune had 64 hostages arrested: the Archbishop of Paris, Darboy, the parish priest of the Madeleine, the entire staff of the Jesuit college, the servants of all the main churches; some had conspired with Versailles, others had tried to save the Church's property from the hands of the Commune. The Archbishop of Paris and the parish priest of the Madeleine wrote to Thiers to support the Commune's request to exchange the 64 hostages for Auguste Blanqui, but the leader of the counter-revolution refused to accept. He knew that with Blanqui he would give the Commune a head. The federates did not shoot a single prisoner, officer, soldier or hostage until 23 May, and this despite the massacre, the assassination of the national guards taken prisoner by Versailles. It was only on 24 May, in tumult and despair, that 52 hostages were executed. The rigours of war were only applied to three spies, and after judgment.

b. The Commune and social classes

The communal revolution represented all the classes that do not live off the work of others. The measures of the Commune, by thwarting the laws of Dufaure, saved the petty-bourgeoisie of shopkeepers, merchants and traders from bankruptcy. The latter had joined the proletarian camp because it recognized that the proletariat was the only one capable of saving it from disaster.

The Commune also addressed itself to the peasants. It told them: "Our victory is your only hope". All the laws made by the party of order between January and February 1850 were avowed measures of repression against the peasants. On 28 April the Commune published a proclamation to the people of the countryside. Only the Commune could resolve in favor of the peasant the problem of the hypothecary debt "lying like an incubus upon his parcel of soil" (M-E, XXII, 338). "The Rurals—this was, in fact, their chief apprehension—knew that three months' free communication of Communal Paris with the provinces would bring about a general rising of the peasants, and hence their anxiety to establish a police blockade around Paris, so as to stop the spread of the rinderpest".

And Marx concluded that "the Commune was thus the true representative of all the healthy elements of French society, and therefore the truly national Government".

c. The national organization of municipalities and centralisation

Marx, in *The Civil War...* (M-E, XXII, 332-333) wrote:

> The Paris Commune was, of course, to serve as a model to all the great industrial centres of France. The communal régime once established in Paris and the secondary centres, the old centralized Government would in the provinces, too, have to give way to the self-government of the producers... the Commune was to be replaced by a national militia, with an extremely short term of service. The rural communes of every district were to administer their common affairs by an assembly of delegates in the central town, and these district assemblies were again to send deputies to the National Delegation in Paris, each delegate to be at any time revocable and bound by the *mandat impératif* (formal instructions) of his constituents. The few but important functions which still would remain for a central government were not to be suppressed... but were to be discharged by Communal, and therefore strictly responsible agents. The unity of the nation was not to be broken, but, on the contrary, to be organized by the Communal constitution... universal suffrage was to serve the people, constituted in Communes, as individual suffrage serves every other employer in the search for the workmen and managers in his business.

d. A new world

The Commune was therefore an acting world, executive and legislative at the same time. It achieved "cheap government" by abolishing these two great sources of expenditure: the standing army and the State civil service. It employed two infallible means to avoid the transformation of a government, servant of society, into master of it: the civil servants were elected by universal suffrage.

Civil servants were also dismissable; the Commune paid for all services only by the wages of other workers, putting a stop to careerism. But all these points were *only the corollary of a final goal: the economic emancipation of labor, the communist society!*

But without having reached this goal, the Commune had already established a new world in Paris!

> Wonderful, indeed, was the change the Commune had wrought in Paris!... "We," said a member of the Commune, "hear no longer of assassination, theft, and personal assault; it seems indeed as if the police had dragged along with it to Versailles all its Conservative friends". The cocottes had refound the scent of their protectors... In their stead, the real women of Paris showed again at the surface—heroic, noble, and devoted, like the women of antiquity. Working, thinking, fighting, bleeding Paris—almost forgetful, in its incubation of a new society, of the cannibals at its gates—radiant in the enthusiasm of its historic initiative! Opposed to this new world at Paris, behold the old world at Versailles—that assembly of the ghouls of all defunct régimes, Legitimists and Orléanists, eager to feed upon the carcass of the nation—with a tail of antediluvian republicans, sanctioning, by their presence in the Assembly, the slave-holders' rebellion... There it was, this Assembly, the representative of everything dead in France... Paris all truth, Versailles all lie; and that lie vented through the mouth of Thiers (M-E, XXII, 341-342).

5. MARX, ENGELS AND THE ATTITUDE OF IWMA TO FRENCH EVENTS

a. The weaknesses of the French workers' movement on the eve of the Commune

As early as 1869, in a letter to Kugelmann of March 3 (M-E, XLIII, 232), Marx wrote: "In France—a very interesting movement in progress. The Parisians are once again really studying their recent revolutionary past, to prepare themselves for the pending new revolutionary business".

And in Engels on 14 July: "I had been for a week ... in Paris where, BY THE BY, a growing movement is manifest" (M-E, XLIII, 317).

Marx and Engels judged this awakening of the French working class without deluding themselves, because the movement remained in the grip of the

Proudhonians and the Blanquists. In spite of the development of the sections of the IWMA in France, they knew that the French workers, still rocked by democratic and nationalist illusions, and who "had just come out of the Lower Empire" (Engels to Marx on 10 August 1870), still had a lot to learn and that it would be madness to want to overthrow Bonaparte at the present time.

Already in 1866, after the 1st Congress of the IWMA in Geneva, Marx, in a letter to Kugelmann on 9 October, spoke of the members of the French section as follows: "The Parisian gentlemen had their heads stuffed full of the most vacuous Proudhonist clichés.... They spurn all revolutionary action, i.e. arising from the class struggle itself, every concentrated social movement, and therefore also that which can be achieved by political means (e.g., such as limitation of the working day by law). Beneath the cloak of freedom and anti-governmentalism or anti-authoritarian individualism these gentlemen, who for 16 years now have so quietly endured the most wretched despotism, and are still enduring it, are in actuality preaching vulgar bourgeois economics, only in the guise of Proudhonist idealism!"(M-E, XLII, 326).

Similarly, on 11th February 1870, in a letter to Marx (M-E, XLIII, 427), Engels denounced the absence of proletarian leaders:

> ...the 'serious' leaders of the movement are, for their part, really comically serious. It is truly marvellous. The SUPPLY of heads, which, until '48 the proletariat obtained from other classes, appears to have dried up completely, and in all countries. The workers seem to be increasingly constrained to do it themselves.

And when the turn taken by military events in the early days of the war made revolution in France appear inevitable, Marx always noted that the French working class was not prepared for the tasks that fell to it, in a letter to Engels of 8 August 1870 (M-E, XLIV, 39):

> If a revolution breaks out in Paris, it is questionable whether they will have the means and the leaders capable of offering serious resistance to the Prussians. One cannot remain blind to the fact that the 20-year-long Bonapartist farce has brought tremendous demoralisation in its wake. One would hardly be justified to rely on revolutionary heroism. What is your opinion?

Engels thought the same when he condemned, in a letter to Marx of 15 August (M-E, XLIV, 46), the chauvinism of a part of the proletariat:

> Badinguet would never have been able to wage this war without the chauvinism of the mass of the French population: the bourgeoisie, the petty bourgeoisie, the peasants and the imperialistic, Haussmannist building-trade proletariat stemming from the peasants, which Bonaparte created in the big towns. Until this chauvinism is knocked on the head, and knocked good and proper, peace between Germany and France is impossible. One might have expected a proletarian revolution to take this work over, but since the war is already on there is no choice for the Germans but to attend to the job themselves and quickly.

And in their correspondence with the French revolutionaries and their analysis of situations, Marx and Engels always feared the chauvinist susceptibilities of the French.

Marx and Engels are thus very pessimistic about the French proletariat, and they defer to the German proletariat. The German working class has, in fact, in recent years, marked more organizational capacity, more receptivity to scientific socialism. The French workers are strong from their revolutionary past, but the absence of scientific theory will make its deplorable effects felt: they are too imbued with democratic prejudices and their representatives (Proudhonians and Blanquists) have not gone beyond the level of utopian socialism.

b. Facing the Franco-Prussian war

Prussian victory would strengthen the German and French proletariats

It is a question for Germany to finally settle the problem of its national unity, thus allowing the German proletariat to organize itself on the national level and thus to have a much more considerable force. Engels, in his letter to Marx of 15 August 1870 (M-E, XLIV, 46), explains it, making it clear, moreover, that what preoccupies Marxists is not the interest of the bourgeoisies but of the national proletariats in this war:

> If Germany wins, French Bonapartism will at any rate be smashed, the endless row about the establishment of German unity will at last be over, the German workers will be able to

organise on a national scale quite different from that prevailing hitherto, and the French workers, whatever sort of government may succeed this one, are certain to have a freer field than under Bonapartism. The whole mass of the German people of every class have realized that this is first and foremost a question of national existence and have therefore at once flung themselves into the fray…

The Prussian victory would thus strengthen not only the German proletariat, but also the French proletariat. Engaging in a war of defense of Germany in formation against French imperialism, helping to defeat Napoleon from outside, was thus for the German workers the practical way to prove their internationalism by helping the French proletariat get rid of the Bonapartist parasite.

A German defensive war

This was also supported in the First Address of the General Council on the Franco-German War of 23 July 1870; and in September 1870 Marx wrote to the Social Democratic Committee in Brunswick: "As long as Napoleon's armies threatened Germany, our duty as Germans was the defensive war, the war for German independence".

Marx and Engels therefore condemned the socialist deputies W. Liebknecht and A. Bebel who advocated abstention; Engels, again on 15 August 1970 (M-E, XLIV, 46), wrote to Marx: "That in these circumstances a German political party should preach total abstention à la Wilhelm and place all sorts of secondary considerations before the main one, seems to me impossible".

Marx explains the case to the General Council of 26 July 1870 (*Documents of the First International*, Vol. 4, 32): "In the North German Parliament, two members of our Association, Liebknecht and Bebel, had abstained from voting the 120,000,000 war loan, giving as their reason, in a written declaration, that they could not vote it because it was a dynastic war and that a vote in favor would imply a vote of confidence in the Prussian Ministry, while a vote against might be interpreted as favoring the criminal designs of Bonaparte".

The Lassallian deputies had voted in favor, and the attitude of the two socialist deputies was met with strong hostility within their own faction, particularly on the part of the executive committee of the socialist democratic workers' party, the Brunswick committee. After the war took an imperialist turn in November 1870, they voted against the credits and were arrested.

Also in his letter to Marx of 15 August 70, Engels had made clear the limits of their support for the defensive war: to join the national movement insofar as it was limited to the defense of Germany; to stress the difference between Germany's national interests and the interests of the dynasty and Prussia; to oppose any annexation of Alsace-Lorraine (a campaign for such annexation was developing in Germany); to act in favor of an honorable peace as soon as a republican government was established in Paris, without chauvinism.

The General Council of London therefore thought it right to give the German workers, when war broke out, the watchword "defense of the fatherland", but on condition that this war did not lose its defensive character, that an honorable peace be concluded with France. Marx, in his Second Address of 9 September 1870 (M-E, XXII, 267), clearly affirmed: "The German working class have resolutely supported the war, which it was not in their power to prevent, as a war for German independence and the liberation of France and Europe from that pestilential incubus, the Second Empire".

And to the Brunswick Committee on 22 August 1870 (M-E, XXII, 261): "If they conclude an honourable peace with France, that war will emancipate Europe from the Muscovite dictatorship, make Prussia merge into Germany, allow the western continent peaceful development and, finally, help a social revolution to break out in Russia, whose elements only need such an impulse from without for their development—thus benefitting the Russian people, too".

Advancing the international labor movement

On 20 July 1870 Marx wrote to Engels (M-E, XLIV, 3-4): "If the Prussians win, then centralisation of the STATE POWER will be beneficial for the centralization of the German working class. German predominance would also transfer the centre of gravity of the workers' movement in Western Europe from France to Germany, and one has only to compare the movement in the two countries from 1866 till now to see that the German working class is superior to the French both theoretically and organizationally. Their predominance over the French on the world stage would also mean the predominance of our theory over Proudhon's, etc.".

This prediction has once again proved to be correct.

Therefore, it is in the interest of the international labor movement that Marx wants to see the German proletariat take the lead in the labor movement in Europe.

This war must not degenerate into an offensive war, i.e. an imperialist war

In the First Address of the General Council to the members of the IWMA in Europe and the US of 22 July 1870 (M-E, XLIV, 6), Marx already warned German workers: "If the German working class allows the present war to lose its strictly defensive character and to degenerate into a war against the French people, victory of defeat will prove alike disastrous. All the miseries that befell Germany after her wars of independence will revive with accumulated intensity".

This prediction, as Engels points out in his introduction of 1891 to *The Civil War...*, proved to be correct with the 20 years of Bismarckian domination, the hunt for socialists, etc...

The Address went on to recall that in the background of this suicidal struggle there was the shadow of Russia, to which Prussia could appeal, once again prostrating Germany at the feet of the tsar.

The task of the German proletariat is therefore to help the French proletariat to liberate itself and not to contribute to its oppression.

c. Marx and Engels and the Paris situation during the war

The collapse of the Empire

"General" Engels, who would write some sixty articles on the Franco-Prussian war, stated on 10 August 1870, after the first defeats of the French armies, in a letter to Marx (M-E, XLIV, 41):

> The bas empire looks like dissolving in a fart. Badinguet is abdicating from the army and has to hand it over to Bazaine (!!) who is now the best man among those left undefeated. This means in reality that he is abdicating altogether. It seems that people are to have the revolution made very easy for them; everything is falling to pieces entirely of its own accord, as was to be expected. The next few days will surely decide the matter. I think that without the army the Orleanists are not strong enough to risk a restoration immediately.

Marx and Engels therefore expect a revolutionary outburst, and even wish for it because the situation is favorable since the bourgeoisie is not ready to react to it. They comment about the rapid decomposition of Bonapartist society, which opened the way for a rapid takeover of Paris by Prussian troops. They therefore envisage the following tactic in Engels' letter to Marx of 15 August 1870 (M-E, XLIV, 48):

The débâcle in France seems to be frightful. Everything squandered, sold, swindled away. The chassepots70 are badly made and misfire in action;... Nevertheless a revolutionary government, if it comes soon, need not despair. But it must abandon Paris to its fate and carry on the war from the South. There would then still be a possibility of its holding out until arms have been bought and new armies organised which would gradually force the enemy back to the frontier. This would really be the true end of the war, both countries reciprocally furnishing proof that they are unconquerable.

And on August 17, 1870, Marx could finally sound the death knell in a letter to Engels(M-E, XLIV, 51): "The Second Empire died as it was born, in parody. This is what I had foreseen with my Bonaparte".

Unfortunately, the revolutionary forces did not intervene and missed the favorable opportunity. On 20 August 1970 (M-E, XLIV, 53) Engels wrote to Marx:

I think that the ANNEXATION of the French Germans is as good as settled. If a revolutionary government had been formed in Paris as late as last week something still might have been done about it. Now, however, it comes too late and can only make a fool of itself by parodying the Convention. I am convinced that Bismarck would have settled for a peace without cession of territory with a revolutionary government if it had come on the scene in time.

Events are rushing.

But all the same, when this becomes known in Paris we must expect something or other to happen. I cannot believe that this flood of news, which is bound to become known today or tomorrow, will fail to produce its effect.

Engels wrote this to Marx on 4 September 1870 (M-E, XLIV, 61-62), the day of the proclamation of the Republic in Paris. And he continues:

The war is at an end. The war is at an end. There is no longer an army in France. As soon as Bazaine capitulates, which will likely as not happen this week, half the German army will march on Paris and the other half across the Loire to sweep the country clean of all armed units.

No sooner said than done!

The Republic of 4 September

Marx and Engels are under no illusions once they get to know the members of the new government. Marx is at a loss for words to denounce Julius Favre's treachery since 1848, and Engels wrote to him on 7 September 1870: "The entire republic, like its pacific origin, has been a complete farce up to now" (M-E, XLIV, 67).

In the Second Address of the General Council on the Franco-Prussian War, Marx was quite clear (M-E, XXII, 268-269):

> ...we hail the advent of the republic in France, but at the same time we labor under misgivings which we hope will prove groundless. That republic has not subverted the throne, but only taken its place, become vacant. It has been proclaimed, not as a social conquest, but as a national measure of defence. It is in the hands of a Provisional Government composed partly of notorious Orleanists, partly of middle class republicans, upon some of whom the insurrection of June 1848 has left its indelible stigma. The division of labor amongst the members of that government looks awkward. The Orleanists have seized the strongholds of the army and the police, while to the professed republicans have fallen the talking departments. Some of their acts go far to show that they have inherited from the empire, not only ruins, but also its dread of the working class.... Is the republic, by some of its middle class undertakers, not intended to serve as a mere stop-gap and bridge over an Orleanist restoration?

Thus, for Marx and Engels, this Republic was not proclaimed as a social conquest, and they feared that it would hide a future Orleanist restoration. They will not be surprised by the national defection of this government, whose lies they will not cease to denounce later on.

Moreover Marx and Engels will castigate the French chauvinism which explodes more and more after the proclamation of the Republic. The Paris office of the IWMA, which on July 15, 1870, had organized a demonstration with the cry "Long live peace!" and published on July 12 a manifesto "To the workers of all countries" in protest against the war that was coming, launched an appeal "To the German people, to the socialist democracy of the German nation" whose chauvinistic tone raised the sarcasm of Marx and Engels. Thus Engels wrote to Marx on September 7 (M-E, XLIV, 66-67):

> If the telegraphed version of the Parisian International procla-mation is anything near accurate, it undoubtedly shows that these people are still entirely dominated by rhetoric. Having endured Badinguet for 20 years, having been unable to prevent him from winning 6 million votes against one and a half only six months ago and from stirring them up against Germany without any rhyme or reason, now that the German victories have made them a present of a republic—et laquelle!—these people demand that the Germans should leave the sacred soil of France without delay, for otherwise there will be guerre à outrance!

Serraillier, a French worker living in London, who had reached Paris on Sep-tember 6, describes the situation of the Parisian internationalists at the General Council as follows (Marx quotes a passage from one of his letters to Caesar de Paepe on September 14, 1870) (M-E, XLIV, 80):

> It is unbelievable that for six years people can be International-ists, abolish frontiers, no longer recognise anyone as a foreign-er, and arrive at the stage they have now reached, simply in order to preserve a factitious popularity to which they will sooner or later fall victim. When I express indignation at their conduct, they tell me that, were they to speak otherwise, they would be sent packing!... Moreover, what a situation they are creating for the International by their ultra-chauvinist dis-courses!... Moreover, what a situation they are creating for the International by their ultra-chauvinist discourses!

In fact, the French sections of the IWMA were disorganized at that time. The trials, the persecutions of the last few years, the mobilization of the war had broken up the workers' organizations. Some militants like Varlin, Theisz, Frankel, Avrial, Combault tried to reconstitute the disorganized or ruined sections. They sought advice from the General Council in London. Marx, in a letter to Engels dated 6 September 1870, states that he "sent a detailed answer today to the Conseil Fédéral, and have also subjected myself to the unpleasant task of opening their eyes to the true state of affairs" (M-E, XLIV, 65).

After Sedan, the war had ceased to be a war for the defense of German national territory. On September 5, the German Social Democratic Committee had launched an appeal inviting the German working class to demonstrate publicly in favor of an honorable peace with the French Republic and against the annexation of Alsace-Lorraine. But on September 9, the signatories of the appeal were apprehended by the military authorities and taken to the fortress of Lötzen in East Prussia.

On the very day of these arrests, the General Council of the IWMA in London expressed itself in a Second Address on September 9, 1870 (M-E, XLIV, 267), written by Marx and partly by Engels to explain the new situation to the working classes of Europe and the USA. The Address denounced the imperialist character of the war that Bismarck and behind him the German bourgeoisie were waging against France. It examines the "allegations" made by the "intrepid patriots" of Germany to justify the annexation of Alsace-Lorraine and explains that this annexation will push the French Republic into the arms of Tsarism:

> If the fortune of her arms, the arrogance of success, and dynastic intrigue lead Germany to a dismemberment of French territory, there will then only remain two courses open to her. She must at all risks become the avowed tool of Russian aggrandizement, or, after some short respite, make again ready for another "defensive" war, not one of those new-fangled "localized" wars, but a war of races—a war with the combined Slavonic and Roman races.

Indeed, the Alsace conquered by Richelieu and the Lorraine bought from Austria in 1735, freed from feudal fetters since 1789 (the Marseillaise was composed in Strasbourg in 1792!) were Francophile, although a German dialect was usually spoken there. The importance of the strategic advantage is the only excuse one can find for the annexation, but the political consequences are serious. The annexation of Alsace-Lorraine makes Russia the arbiter of Europe. By wresting from France its two fanatically patriotic provinces, Russia was pushed into the arms of anyone who would open the prospect of their recovery, and France was made an eternal enemy. And against Germany, France's natural ally is Russia. If the two largest nations of the Western continent neutralize each other with an eternal bone of contention that drives them to fight each other, Russia will have freer hands to maneuver.

German workers must therefore demand an honorable peace for France and the recognition of the French Republic.

As for the French workers, they find themselves in a very difficult situation with this Republic proclaimed not as a social conquest but as a measure of national defense, which may moreover hide an Orleanist maneuver in view of the monarchical restoration. And the Address strongly advises the French working class against overthrowing the new government(M-E, XXII, 269):

> Any attempt at upsetting the new Government in the present crisis, when the enemy is almost knocking at the doors of Paris, would be a desperate folly. The French workmen must perform their duties as citizens; but, at the same time, they must not allow themselves to be deluded by the national souvenirs of 1792, as the French peasants allowed themselves to be deluded by the national souvenirs of the First Empire.... Let them calmly and resolutely improve the opportunities of republican liberty, for the work of their own class organisation. It will gift them with fresh herculean powers for the regeneration of France, and our common task—the emancipation of labour. Upon their energies and wisdom hinges the fate of the republic.

Insurrection would therefore be madness!

And Marx and Engels to denounce nationalist illusions. "Fighting against the Prussians for the benefit of the bourgeoisie would be madness" as Engels wrote to Marx on September 12, 1870. In the same letter, he says that the workers should be prevented from starting a peace movement, for if they were to win now in the service of national defense, they would have to assume the legacy of Bonaparte and the present miserable republic, and, since they would inevitably be defeated by the German armies, they would be rejected twenty years later. With peace, the government loses any chance of lasting long: all the chances for the workers would be more favorable than they were before. Engels deplores the fact that in Paris there are so few people who have the courage to consider the situation as it really is.

From the Republic to the Commune

During the whole period from the proclamation of the Republic to that of the Commune, Marx and Engels with the General Council will do everything possible to help the French working class. Through Lafargue, Serraillier and others, they multiplied the organizational advice to the workers and denounced the sabotage of national defense by the bourgeoisie.

Marx will also launch in England a campaign for the recognition of the Republic in France by the British government to counter the threat of a restoration of the Orleans.

d. The IWMA and the Commune

Parisian internationals

As noted above, the situation of the French sections was bad, and moreover the General Council in London was hostile to an insurrection. The Parisian internationals initially showed some reservations about the CC of the National Guard and hesitated to get involved in its action. On 1 March, at the meeting of the IWMA Federal Council, Varlin, foreseeing the events that were to take place, did not want the section to be uninvolved and asked that the internationals do their best to be appointed as delegates in the companies of the National Guard and to sit on the CC. Varlin cried out: "Let's go there not as internationals but as National Guards and work to capture the spirit of this assembly!" But the Federal Council remains hesitant; Frankel answers: "This looks like a compromise with the bourgeoisie, I don't want it!" The Council nevertheless decided to delegate to the CC of the National Guard a commission of four members whose action was to be purely individual and not to compromise the International. Four internationals (Babick, Varlin, Assi, Alavoine) will thus be part of the CC.

As a result, the International, even though it will be accused of being the instigator (Assi, a member of the Paris office had his name, because of the alphabetical order, placed at the head of the proclamations!), participated very little and contributed little to the production of the day of March 18. On 22 March, the members of the Federal Council wished to emphasize that the International is "free of any responsibility" vis-à-vis the CC. Only at the session of 23–24 March will the Federal Chamber of Workers' Societies and the Federal Council of the IWMA strengthen the CC with all their moral force and publish a manifesto in which they affirm, among other things, that "the communal delegation is the guarantee of the emancipation of the workers".

First of all, they do not see in 18 March a revolutionary movement; thus, Varlin replied to the letter from Bakunin and Guillaume, who saw in 18 March the Universal Social Revolution "that it was not an international revolution, that the 18 March movement had no other goal than to demand municipal franchises in Paris and that this goal had been achieved; that the elections were set for the following day and that once the municipal council was elected, the CC would resign its powers and everything would be over". There was nothing subversive about such a program.

Afterwards, the internationals would try to give the communist movement a program, guidelines; they would, among other things, take charge of the economic and social program in the Commune through the Labor Commission.

Here is the content of some of the meetings of the Federal Council of the IWMA: on March 29, appointment of an intermediate commission between the Council and the Commune; on April 12, unanimous expulsion of Tolain, who sided with the Versailles people, and proposal to the General Council of London to sanction this expulsion (which it did on April 29); on May 8: to the Carrières and Montmartre section of the International, a motion for compulsory and free primary and professional lay education at all levels; 20 May: at the extraordinary session of the Federal Council of the Parisian sections of the IWMA, the members of the International who are members of the Commune are invited to make "every effort to maintain the unity of the Commune".

Marx, Engels and the London General Council

In the preface to the collection of letters to Kugelman, Lenin wrote: "In September 1870 Marx had called the insurrection an act of desperate folly; but in April 1871, when he saw the mass movement of the people, he watched it with the keen attention of a participant in great events marking a step forward in the historic revolutionary movement" (Lenin, XII, 109).

And Marx wrote to Kugelmann on April 17, 1871(M-E, XLIV, 137):

> But of this, the bourgeois canaille of Versailles were also well aware. Precisely for that reason they presented the Parisians with the alternative of taking up the fight or succumbing without a struggle. In the latter case, the demoralisation of the working class would have been a far greater misfortune than the fall of any number of "leaders" (Kugelmann had written to Marx that defeat would again deprive the workers of their leaders). The struggle of the working class against the capitalist class and its state has entered upon a new phase with the struggle in Paris. Whatever the immediate results may be, a

new point of departure of world-historic importance has been gained.

Lenin continues:

> But, when the masses rose, Marx wanted to march with them, to learn with them in the process of the struggle, and not to give them bureaucratic admonitions. He realised that to attempt in advance to calculate the chances with complete accuracy would be quackery or hopeless pedantry. What he valued above everything else was that the working class heroically and self-sacrificingly took the initiative in making world history. Marx regarded world history from the standpoint of those who make it without being in a position to calculate the chances infallibly beforehand, and not from the standpoint of an intellectual philistine who moralises: "It was easy to foresee... they should not have taken up..." Marx was also able to appreciate that there are moments in history when a desperate struggle of the masses, even for a hopeless cause, is essential for the further schooling of these masses and their training for the next struggle (Lenin, XII ,111).

Marx therefore followed the Parisian events very closely with the General Council. The General Council even intervened by delegating two French workers, Dupont and Serraillier, who will be elected to the Commune during the complementary elections of April 16. Serraillier will even be part of the Labor Commission. It is thanks to them, to Léo Frankel, to Lafargue who arrived from Bordeaux to Paris on April 6, 1871, that the London General Council was kept informed. Marx also had other correspondents: the Proudhonian Charles Longuet, the Blanquists E. Vaillant, E. Varlin, Vermorel, E. Dmitrieff (from Geneva, she left for Paris at the beginning of March 1871, charged with a mission of information). And Marx wrote many letters to Varlin and Frankel who asked her for advice.

On April 28 (M-E, XLIV, 148–149), he wrote to Frankel about the slanders that F. Pyat was spreading about Serraillier and Dupont, and on May 13 to Frankel and Varlin:

> Might it not be useful if all papers likely to compromise the riffraff of Versailles were kept in a safe place? A precaution of

this kind could never do any harm.... I have written hundreds of letters on behalf of your cause to all the corners of the earth where we have branches... I believe that the Commune wastes too much time over trifles and personal squabbles. One can see that there are influences at work other than those of the working men. None of this would matter if you had time enough to make up for lost time....after the definitive conclusion of peace [the Prussians] will allow the government to invest Paris with its gendarmes... Since the prior condition for the accomplishment of their treaty was the conquest of Paris, they asked Bismarck to delay payment of the first instalment until the occupation of Paris. Bismarck accepted this condition. Prussia, being herself in urgent need of that money, will therefore provide the Versailles people with every possible facility to hasten the occupation of Paris. So be on your guard!

Most of the letters written by Marx could not be found. In them, Marx touched on very important questions, of a financial nature in order to provide the Commune with material means, of a military nature in order to defend the Commune, and of a political nature to warn it against avowed or camouflaged enemies and to advise it on this or that social measure.

In a letter of June 12, 1871 (M-E, XLIV, 151), Marx explains to Beesly his relations with the Commune:

My relations with the Commune were maintained through a German merchant who travels between Paris and London all the year round. Everything was settled verbally with the exception of two matters: First, through the same intermediary, I sent the members of the Commune a letter in answer to a question from them as to how they could handle certain securities on the London Exchange. Second, on May 11, ten days before the catastrophe, I sent them by the same method all the details of the secret agreement come to between Bismarck and Favre in Frankfort. I had this information from Bismarck's right hand--a man who had formerly (from 1848–53) belonged to the secret society of which I was the leader... If only the Commune had listened to my warnings! I advised its members to fortify the northern side of the heights of Montmartre, the Prussian side, and they still had time to do this; I told them beforehand that they would otherwise be caught in a trap; I denounced Pyat, Grousset and Vesinier to them; I demanded that they should at once send to London all the documents compromising the members of the National Defence, so that by this means the savagery of the enemies of the Commune could to some extent be held in check—thus the plan of the Versailles people would have been brought to nothing. If these documents had been discovered by the Versailles people they would not have published forged ones.

The Commune is the daughter of the International

Marx wrote to Kugelman on 12 April 1871 (M-E, XLIV, 132): "...the present rising in Paris—even if it be crushed by the wolves, swine and vile curs of the old society—is the most glorious deed of our Party since the June Insurrection in Paris".

And Engels to Sorge in September 1874 (M-E, XLV, 41): "The Commune was without any doubt the child of the International intellectually, although the International did not lift a finger to produce it".

They had the right to claim the Commune as an achievement of our party, because the working class was the backbone of the movement and the Parisian members of the International were among the most far-sighted elements of the Commune.

e. Rearguard Fighting

After the Commune, the fear of the international bourgeoisie, haunted by the spectre of communism, was unleashed with its terrorism against the workers, the communards, and the members of the IWMA. This repression took the form of denunciation, forgery, defamation and falsification of the principles and goals of the Commune and socialism. The IWMA, under the leadership of Marx and Engels, struck back with the means at its disposal to ensure that both the Commune and the Association were respected everywhere. Marx declared on September 21, 1871 (M-E, XXII, 618): "As Vaillant proposes, we must challenge all governments everywhere, even in Switzerland, in response to their persecution of the International. The reaction exists on every continent; it is general and permanent, even in the United States and England in another form".

And for this, Marx and Engels spent an incredible amount of energy, as Marx's wife attests in a letter of May 26, 1872 to W. Liebknecht:

> You cannot imagine what we have had to endure here in London since the fall of the Commune. All the nameless misery, the suffering without end! And on top of that, the almost unbearable work on behalf of the International. As long as Moor had all the work and just managed, thanks to his diplomacy and tactical skill, to keep the various unruly elements together in the face of the world and the cohorts of enemies, as long as he succeeded in sparing the Association RIDICULE, inspired the trembling crew with fear and terror... he has no peace by day or by night (M-E, XLIV, 580).

And in the same way Marx and Engels fought like lions to help the communal refugees in London. Thus Marx's daughter, Jenny Longuet, in a letter to Kugelmann of December 21, 1871 (M-E, XLIV, 565–566) describes the situation as follows:

> For the last three weeks I have been running from one suburb of London to the other...and then I have often written letters until one o'clock in the morning. The object of these journeys and letters is to obtain funds for the support of the refugees... For more than five months the International has now supported, that is to say, has held between life and death the great mass of exiles...you can imagine how much these difficulties torture our poor Moor.

6. PROLETARIAN REVOLUTION, COMMUNIST REVOLUTION

"The Paris Commune of 1871 was the first, as yet weak, historic attempt of the working class to impose its supremacy" (Trotsky, Terrorism and Communism).

a. Proletarian State

Working-class government

Engels, in his introduction to *The Civil War...* (M-E, XXVII, 180) of 1891, speaks of the insurrectional movements since 1789 which have always had a proletarian character in France: "The economic development of France since 1789 has meant that for 50 years no revolution has been able to break out without taking on a proletarian character, so that after the victory, the proletariat... entered the scene with its own demands".

But these demands called into question the newly established social order; so the bourgeoisie hastened to disarm the workers: this is what happened in 1848. The new feature of the revolution of 1871: "It is that the people after the first uprising did not disarm themselves and did not put their power in the hands of the republican acrobats of the ruling classes; it is that, through the formation of the Commune, they took in their own hands the effective direction of the revolution".

In fact, the war with Prussia, the betrayal of its bourgeoisie, the unemployment of the proletariat and the ruin of the petty-bourgeoisie pushed the population of Paris to the revolution of March 18, which unexpectedly put the power in the hands of the National Guard, in the hands of the working class and the petty-bourgeoisie, which had sided with it and recognized it as the only one capable of saving Paris from disaster and France from annihilation, the only one capable of social initiative. The only dynamic healthy class, revolutionary in its essence, was the proletariat. But this class cannot be satisfied with the bourgeois Republic that it realizes by going beyond its limits, by already aiming at breaking this bourgeois world that is happy with just seizing power.

"But in modern society, enslaved economically by capital, the proletariat cannot dominate politically unless it breaks the chains which fetter it to capital" (Lenin, XVII, 124). That is to say, to destroy the economic bases on which the existence of the classes is based. In this way labor will be emancipated from exploitation; *The Civil War...* states that the workers government of the Commune is "the bold champion of the emancipation of labor", that productive labor will cease to be the attribute of a class, the proletariat, and that Man, as a generic being, will be freed from the servitude of the exploited and the exploiter. *Every man will finally be only a worker.*

The Commune is already no longer a State.

Marx evoking the Commune (M-E, XXII, 334–335), writes:

> ...it was a thoroughly expansive political form, while all the previous forms of government had been emphatically repressive. Its true secret was this: It was essentially a working class government, the product of the struggle of the producing

against the appropriating class, the political form at last discovered under which to work out the economical emancipation of labour. Except on this last condition, the Communal Constitution would have been an impossibility and a delusion. The political rule of the producer cannot co-exist with the perpetuation of his social slavery. The Commune was therefore to serve as a lever for uprooting the economical foundation upon which rests the existence of classes, and therefore of class rule. With labor emancipated, every man becomes a working man, and productive labor ceases to be a class attribute.

Thus, this workers' government is no longer a State, as Lenin, with the help of Engels, points out: "Since the end of the nineteenth century, however, revolutionary epochs have advanced a higher type of democratic state, a state which in certain respects, as Engels put it, ceases to be a state, is 'no longer a state in the proper sense of the word'. This is a state of the Paris Commune type" (Lenin, XXIV, 68).

For what this proletarian government offers is communism: "Yes, gentlemen, the Commune intended to abolish that class property which makes the labor of the many the wealth of the few. It aimed at the expropriation of the expropriators. It wanted to make individual property a truth by transforming the means of production, land, and capital, now chiefly the means of enslaving and exploiting labor, into mere instruments of free and associated labor" (M-E, XXII, 335).

The insurgents, a majority of workers

Many workers or representatives of workers sat in the Commune. Engels, in his introduction to *The Civil War...* (M-E, XXVII, 185), of 1891 writes:

> Thus, from March 18 onwards the class character of the Paris movement, which had previously been pushed into the background by the fight against the foreign invaders, emerged sharply and clearly. As almost without exception, workers, or recognized representatives of the workers, sat in the Commune, its decision bore a decidedly proletarian character. Either they decreed reforms which the republican bourgeoisie had failed to pass solely out of cowardice, but which provided a necessary basis for the free activity of the working class—such as the realization of the principle that in relation to the

state, religion is a purely private matter—or they promulgated
decrees which were in the direct interests of the working class
and to some extent cut deeply into the old order of society

Moreover, as we have already pointed out above, the insurgents were mostly workers. On the other hand, the proletarian character of the Paris revolution was expressed not only at the level of the Commune, the expression of the proletarian revolution, but also at the level of popular organizations such as the "red" clubs, where all revolutionaries discussed general problems of organization and defense; such as the women's groups organized by Elisabeth Dmitrieff; and such as the vigilance committees of each district which organized the defense and supply of the working class neighborhoods: In Montmartre, Louise Michel, a vibrant heroine of the Commune, who was deported after May, recounts that: "the vigilance committees of Montmartre left no one without shelter, without bread… For those who needed it, the resources of the town hall were not spared, nor were revolutionary means and requisitions. The 18th arrondissement was the terror of the monopolizers. When they said: Montmartre will come down! The reactionaries were digging themselves into their holes, and like chased beasts, they dropped the caches where food was rotting while Paris was starving".

What a beautiful example of proletarian dictatorship!

b. A democratic dictatorship

The error that cannot be imputed to the Commune is that the proletariat accepted to govern with the petty-bourgeoisie. Lenin explains it this way: "…for representatives of the socialist proletariat to take part in a revolutionary government together with the petty bourgeoisie is fully permissible in principle, and, in certain conditions, even obligatory. It shows us further that the real task the Commune had to perform was primarily the achievement of the democratic and not the socialist dictatorship, the implementation of our 'minimum program'" (Lenin, IX, 141).

In fact, the Paris Commune could only win by making the link with the peasantry: "When he is disappointed in the Napoleonic Restoration, the French peasant will part with his belief in his smallholding, the entire state edifice erected on this smallholding will fall to the ground and the proletarian revolution will obtain that chorus without which its solo becomes a swan song in all peasant countries" (M-E, XLIV, 193).

c. The Dictatorship of the Proletariat

Lenin, speaking of the proletarian State, whose type for him is that of the Paris Commune, writes: "Such power is a dictatorship, i. e., it rests not on law, not on the formal will of the majority, but on direct, open force. Force is the instrument of power" (Lenin, XXIV, 239)

But was it so for the Commune? Was there in 1871 a dictatorship of the proletariat in Paris, as Engels apostrophized to the social-democratic philistine: "Look at the Paris Commune, it was the dictatorship of the proletariat!" (M-E, XXVII, 191).

Trotsky, in *Terrorism and Communism*, writes in 1920, in the chapters entitled "The Paris Commune and the Russia of the Soviets" and "Marx and Kautsky" , which answers to the renegade Kautsky who makes of the Paris Commune a model of workers' government, certainly, but... democratic and pacifist as, according to him, it must be, denying thus the dictatorial power of the Soviets: "he sees the predominant qualities of the Commune where we see its misfortunes and its wrongs"!

Dictatorial measures

To Kautsky, who wants to oppose the magnanimity of the Communards to the intransigence of the Bolsheviks, Trotsky, quoting Lavrov who wrote a book on the Commune, retorts: "Just the men, who hold human life and human blood dear must strive to organize the possibility for a swift and decisive victory, and then to act with the greatest swiftness and energy, in order to crush the enemy. For only in this way can we achieve the minimum of inevitable sacrifice and the minimum of bloodshed".

And Trotsky goes on to cite the dictatorial measures that the Commune, moved by necessity, had to take or at least outline:

> Driven by the logic of the struggle, it took its stand in principle on the path of intimidation. The creation of the Committee of Public Safety was dictated, in the case of many of its supporters, by the idea of the Red Terror. The Committee was appointed "to cut off the heads of traitors" "to avenge treachery". Under the head of "intimidatory" decrees we must class the order to seize the property of Thiers and of his ministers to destroy Thiers' house, to destroy the Vendôme column, and especially the decree on hostages. For every captured Communard or

sympathizer with the Commune shot by the Versaillais, three hostages were to be shot. The activity of the Prefecture of Paris controlled by Raoul Rigault had a purely terroristic, though not always a useful, purpose. The effect of all these measures of intimidation was paralyzed by the helpless opportunism of the guiding elements in the Commune, by their striving to reconcile the bourgeoisie with the fait accompli by the help of pitiful phrases, by their vacillations between the fiction of democracy and the reality of dictatorship.

Further on, Trotsky quotes Marx on the hostage issue: "When Thiers, as we have seen, from the very beginning of the conflict, established the very humane practice of shooting the communards who were prisoners, the Commune, in order to protect their lives, had no other resource than to resort to the Prussian practice of taking hostages... How could their lives have been spared any longer, after the carnage with which the praetorians of Mac Mahon had celebrated their entry into Paris".

The Central Committee is afraid of its responsibilities

On March 19, the march on Versailles and the elections to the Commune were proposed to the Central Committee. However, to undertake the march on Versailles, it was necessary to reorganize the National Guard, postpone the elections, and establish a more military regime in the capital. Trotsky quotes Lavrov again: "They had to fight against many internal foes with whom Paris was full, who only yesterday had been rioting around the Exchange and the Vendôme Square, who had their representatives in the administration and in the National Guard, who possessed their press, and their meetings, who almost openly maintained contact with the Versaillais, and who became more determined and more audacious at every piece of carelessness, at every check of the Commune".

At the same time, revolutionary measures of a financial and economic nature had to be taken to satisfy the needs of the revolutionary army. The task of the CC was not to run after legality, but to deal a mortal blow to the enemy. The CC's aspirations for a "legal" government were in fact dictated by fear of responsibility, according to Trotsky, because after the Commune elections the CC would continue to interfere in all affairs, especially military affairs, defying the legality it had so long sought.

Living denial of formal democracy

What was the situation of the democratic Commune and the revolutionary dictatorship?

Again according to Trotsky, the Commune, as much by tradition as by the intentions of its ruling party—the Blanquists—was the expression of the dictatorship of the revolutionary city over the country, over peasant France. It was so in the great French revolution; it would have been the same in the revolution of 1871, if the Commune had not fallen so quickly.

First in Paris, the elections were held after the flight of the bourgeoisie supporting Thiers, and those who remained in Paris nevertheless feared the revolutionary battalions. In fact, the CC, despite a soft and inconsistent dictatorship, attempted to implement the principle of universal suffrage, even if it did not want to. After the elections, the bourgeois elements, conscious of the balance of power in favor of the workers, quickly withdrew from the Commune. Trotsky recalls that in November 1917, during the elections for a Commune on the basis of the most "democratic" suffrage, with no restrictions for the bourgeoisie, the latter boycotted the elections, and the Commune elected with a revolutionary majority nevertheless submitted itself to the Soviet of St. Petersburg, that is to say, it put the dictatorship of the proletariat above the "principle" of universal suffrage.

While the bourgeoisie was under pressure from the events during the elections and despite the revolutionaries, these elections actually reflected the hope for a peaceful agreement with Versailles. The revolutionary leaders wanted agreement, not struggle. The masses had not yet exhausted their illusions: "We must dominate our enemies by moral force..." preached Vermorel, and again: "We must not touch the freedom and life of the individual". Longuet, in the *Journal Officiel* wrote the same thing on April 3: "All dissidence today will disappear because everyone feels solidarity, because there has never been less hatred, less social antagonism".

This fiction of equality, which led people to believe that the question could be resolved without a struggle, even turned into a macabre farce with the 16 April complementary elections. Arthur Arnould wrote: "The vote was no longer an issue. The situation had become tragic... All the men loyal to the Commune were on the fortifications, in the forts, in the outposts. The people attached no importance to these supplementary elections... The time had come not to count the voters, but to have soldiers; not to find out whether we had grown or shrunk in the opinion of Paris, but to defend Paris against the Versaillais".

Only a few elements were aware of the role that the Commune should have played. Thus Millière wrote: "The Commune is not a Constituent Assembly, it is a council of war. It must have only one goal: victory; only one weapon: force; only one law: that of public salvation". Lissagaray adds: "The leaders of the Commune have never been able to understand that it was a barricade and not an administration".

In spite of all these errors, the Commune was the living negation of formal democracy, because in its development it signified the dictatorship of the Parisian workers over the peasant nation. Every action of the Commune was sufficient to convince of its illegal nature.

The Commune, a Parisian municipality, repealed the National Conscription, named its organ the *Official Journal of the French Republic*, touched—albeit too timidly—the Bank of France, proclaimed the separation of Church and State, entered into relations with foreign embassies, etc. All this she did in the name of the revolutionary dictatorship of Paris, without the authorization of national democracy, which had found a more "legal" expression in the Assembly of the Rural People.

7. THE LESSONS OF THE PARIS COMMUNE

a. Proletarian revolution must break the bourgeois State machine. The Commune has shown what it should be replaced by

This thesis was wonderfully and limpidly treated by Lenin in *The State and the Revolution* based on Marx's *The Eighteenth Brumaire*.

Assessment of the class struggles from 1848 to 1851

Marx shows us, in the last chapter of *The 18th Brumaire* (M-E, XI, 183), that the immediate goal of the February revolution was the overthrow of the Orleans dynasty and the fraction of the bourgeoisie that dominated under it, but it is only on December 2, 1851 that this goal was achieved. Indeed, in the parliamentary republic, the domination of the bourgeoisie, after having united all its elements and made its domain the domain of its class, appeared in all its nakedness: "…the revolution had first created the form in which the rule of the bourgeois class received its broadest, most general and ultimate expression and could therefore also be overthrown, without being able to rise again".

And it was then, on December 2, that the sentence pronounced in February against the Orleans bourgeoisie, that is, the most lively fraction of the French bourgeoisie, was carried out. With Louis Bonaparte, it was beaten in its parliament, in its university, its press, its literature, its administrative revenues, "in spirit and in flesh".

On December 2, therefore, it was the victory of the executive power over the legislative, and, as Napoleon was the executor of the February revolution, Guizot (who embodies the politics of the conservative upper bourgeoisie), whom Marx was able to quote, speaking of the coup d'état, was able to exclaim: "It is the complete and definitive triumph of socialism"! But the revolution had played only its first act, as Marx explains it magnificently (M-E, XI, 185–186):

> ...the revolution is thoroughgoing. It is still traveling through purgatory. It does its work methodically. By December 2, 1851, it had completed half of its preparatory work; now it is completing the other half. It first completed the parliamentary power in order to be able to overthrow it. Now that it has achieved this, it completes the executive power, reduces it to its purest expression, isolates it, sets it up against itself as the sole target, in order to concentrate all its forces of destruction against it. And when it has accomplished this second half of its preliminary work, Europe will leap from its seat and exult: Well burrowed, old mole!".

Marx later writes: "Only under the second Bonaparte does the state seem to have made itself completely independent. The state machinery has so strengthened itself vis-à-vis civil society that the Chief of the Society of December 10 suffices for its head".

Marx thus speaks of the forces of destruction to be concentrated on the executive power, that executive power whose history he gives us leads us to the conclusion of its destruction:

> The executive power with its enormous bureaucratic and military organization, with its wide-ranging and ingenious state machinery, with a host of officials numbering half a million, besides an army of another half million—this terrifying parasitic body which enmeshes the body of French society and chokes all its pores sprang up in the time of the absolute

monarchy, with the decay of the feudal system which it had helped to hasten.

Marx thus says that one arrives at a State power "whose work is divided and centralized as in a factory" (M-E, XI, 185).

And finally, we come to the passage of *18th Brumaire* commented on by Lenin, in which Marx speaks of breaking the State machine: "the parliamentary republic, in its struggle against the revolution, found itself compelled to strengthen the means and the centralization of governmental power with repressive measures. All revolutions perfected this machine instead of smashing it" (Lenin, XXV, 411).

Lenin comments luminously on this passage in *The State and the Revolution* (XXV, 411–414):

> In this remarkable argument, Marxism takes a tremendous step forward compared with the *Communist Manifesto*. In the latter, the question of the state is still treated in an extremely abstract manner, in the most general terms and expressions. In the above-quoted passage, the question is treated in a concrete manner, and the conclusion is extremely precise, definite, practical and palpable: all previous revolutions perfected the state machine, whereas it must be broken, smashed. This conclusion is the chief and fundamental point in the Marxist theory of the state.... The question as to how, from the point of view of historical development, the replacement of the bourgeois by the proletarian state is to take place is not raised here (in the *Communist Manifesto*).

> This is the question Marx raises and answers in 1852. True to his philosophy of dialectical materialism, Marx takes as his basis the historical experience of the great years of revolution, 1848 to 1851. Here, as everywhere else, his theory is a summing up of experience, illuminated by a profound philosophical conception of the world and a rich knowledge of history

> The problem of the state is put specifically: How did the bourgeois state, the state machine necessary for the rule of the bourgeoisie, come into being historically?... The centralized state power that is peculiar to bourgeois society came into be-

ing in the period of the fall of absolutism. Two institutions most characteristic of this state machine are the bureaucracy and the standing army... This course of events compels the revolution *"to concentrate all its forces of destruction"* against the state power, and to set itself the aim, not of improving the state machine, but of *smashing and destroying it.*

It was not logical reasoning, but actual developments, the actual experience of 1848–51, that led to the matter being presented in this way. The extent to which Marx held strictly to the solid ground of historical experience can be seen from the fact that, in 1852, he did not yet specifically raise the question of what was to take the place of the state machine to be destroyed. Experience had not yet provided material for dealing with this question, which history placed on the agenda later on, in 1871. In 1852, all that could be established with the accuracy of scientific observation was that the proletarian revolution had approached the task of "concentrating all its forces of destruction" against the state power, of "smashing" the state machine.

Destruction of the State machine

Thus, with Napoleon III, the State machine threw down the parliamentary mask and reached the maximum of its concentration, thus facilitating the work of the proletarian revolution. The period 1848–51 had shown that the proletarian revolution had to exercise a dictatorship, that is, a power based on the repression of the old ruling class, and on the other hand that it could not use the bourgeois State machine. The Commune verified this analysis; as early as April 12, 1871, Marx wrote to Kugelmann (M-E, XLIV, 131):

> If you look at the last chapter of my *Eighteenth Brumaire* you will find that I say that the next attempt of the French revolution will be no longer, as before, to transfer the bureaucratic military machine from one hand to another, but to break it, and that is essential for every real people's revolution on the Continent. And this is what our heroic Party comrades in Paris are attempting.

And he repeats it in *The Civil War...*: "The working class cannot be satisfied with taking the State machine as it is and making it work for its own account".

The political form found to replace the bourgeois State machine

And we can exclaim, with Marx and Lenin, that the substitution of new, proletarian organs for the old ones is *"the greatest step forward of the world proletarian movement"*.

Lenin, taking up the motto of Marx in his *The 18 Brumaire*, "to break the bureaucratic and military machine," comments: "in these few words is briefly expressed the main lesson of Marxism about the tasks of the proletariat towards the State during the Revolution" (XXV, 420). The Paris Commune tried to accomplish this task, and it would have accomplished it —f it had had the time— in alliance with the peasantry (hence the expression "popular revolution" used by Marx in his letter to Kugelman of April 12, 1871), an alliance towards which it made its way.

Characteristics of the proletarian State

"Since the end of the nineteenth century, however, revolutionary epochs have advanced a higher type of democratic state, a state which in certain respects, as Engels put it, ceases to be a state, is 'no longer a state in the proper sense of the word'" (Letter from Engels to Bebel on the Gotha program of March 18–28, 1875). "This is a state of the Paris Commune type" (Lenin, XXIV, 68).

And again: "Such power is a dictatorship, i. e., it rests not on law, not on the formal will of the majority, but on direct, open force" (Lenin. XXIV, 239).

Apart from these two fundamental characteristics of the proletarian State, let's look at the general measures:

1. Suppression of bureaucracy.

2. Abolition of the permanent army.

3. Suppression of the power of the Church.

4. National organization.

Suppression of the civil service and the standing army.

Engels, in his introduction to *The Civil War...* (M-E, XXVII, 189–190) wrote:

> From the outset the Commune was compelled to recognize that the working class, once come to power, could not go on managing with the old state machine; that in order not to lose again its only just conquered supremacy, this working class must, on the one hand, do away with all the old repressive machinery

previously used against it itself, and, on the other, safeguard itself against its own deputies and officials, by declaring them all, without exception, subject to recall at any moment... Against this transformation of the state and the organs of the state from servants of society into masters of society—an inevitable transformation in all previous states—the Commune made use of two infallible expedients. In this first place, it filled all posts—administrative, judicial, and educational—by election on the basis of universal suffrage of all concerned, with the right of the same electors to recall their delegate at any time. And in the second place, all officials, high or low, were paid only the wages received by other workers. The highest salary paid by the Commune to anyone was 6,000 francs. In this way an effective barrier to place-hunting and careerism was set up, even apart from the binding mandates to delegates to representative bodies which were added besides.

Lenin remarks, again in *The State and the Revolution*: "the transition from capitalism to socialism is impossible without a certain 'reversion' to 'primitive' democracy...based on capitalism" (Lenin, XXV, 425).

As for the army, Paris

got rid of the army, and replaced it by a National Guard, the bulk of which consisted of working men. This fact was now to be transformed into an institution. The first decree of the Commune, therefore, was the suppression of the standing army, and the substitution for it of the armed people.... The Commune was to be a working, not a parliamentary body, executive and legislative at the same time. Instead of continuing to be the agent of the Central Government, the police was at once stripped of its political attributes, and turned into the responsible, and at all times revocable, agent of the Commune. (*The Civil War...*)

And thus "The Commune made that catchword of bourgeois revolutions—cheap government—a reality by destroying the two greatest sources of expenditure: the standing army and state functionarism".

With regard to the suppression of the power of the Church, Lenin notes in *The State and the Revolution*, that religion is only a private matter in relation to the State and not in relation to the party. And Marx comments on this general measure of the Commune:

> Having once got rid of the standing army and the police—the physical force elements of the old government—the Commune was anxious to break the spiritual force of repression, the "parson-power", by the disestablishment and disendowment of all churches as proprietary bodies. The priests were sent back to the recesses of private life, there to feed upon the alms of the faithful in imitation of their predecessors, the apostles. The whole of the educational institutions were opened to the people gratuitously, and at the same time cleared of all interference of church and state. Thus, not only was education made accessible to all, but science itself freed from the fetters which class prejudice and governmental force had imposed upon it.

It was not a question of directly tackling spiritual oppression—which would only have strengthened it—but of removing its material basis.

On the question of national organization and the abolition of parliamentarianism, it is still Marx who speaks:

> The Paris Commune was, of course, to serve as a model to all the great industrial centres of France. The communal regime once established in Paris and the secondary centres, the old centralized government would in the provinces, too, have to give way to the self-government of the producers. In a rough sketch of national organization, which the Commune had no time to develop, it states clearly that the Commune was to be the political form of even the smallest country hamlet, and that in the rural districts the standing army was to be replaced by a national militia, with an extremely short term of service. The rural communities of every district were to administer their common affairs by an assembly of delegates in the central town, and these district assemblies were again to send deputies to the National Delegation in Paris, each delegate to be at any time revocable and bound by the mandat imperatif (formal instructions) of his constituents. The few but important functions which would still remain for a central government were not to be suppressed, as has been intentionally misstated, but

were to be discharged by Communal and thereafter responsible agents. The unity of the nation was not to be broken, but, on the contrary, to be organized by Communal Constitution, and to become a reality by the destruction of the state power which claimed to be the embodiment of that unity...from which it was but a parasitic excrescence.

As for parliamentarism, Marx settles it as follows:

Instead of deciding once in three or six years which member of the ruling class was to misrepresent the people in Parliament, universal suffrage was to serve the people, constituted in Communes, as individual suffrage serves every other employer in the search for the workmen and managers in his business. And it is well-known that companies, like individuals, in matters of real business generally know how to put the right man in the right place, and, if they for once make a mistake, to redress it promptly. On the other hand, nothing could be more foreign to the spirit of the Commune than to supersede universal suffrage by hierarchical investiture.

There is no trace of Proudhon or Bakunin-style federalism!

Conclusion

Lenin sums up the characteristics of the proletarian State. Speaking about the proletarian power of 1917, he writes (XXIV, 38–39):

This power is of the same type as the Paris Commune, a type whose main characteristics are as follows:

1- The source of power is not the law previously discussed and voted on by a Parliament, but the initiative of the popular masses, a direct, local initiative, coming from below, a direct 'coup de force', to use a common expression.

2- The police and the army, institutions separate from the people and opposed to the people, are replaced by the direct arming of the whole people; under this power, it is the workers and armed peasants, it is the armed people themselves who ensure the maintenance of public order.

3- The body of civil servants, the bureaucracy, are also replaced by the direct power of the people, or at least placed under special control; not only do the posts become elective, but their holders, reduced to the status of simple representatives, can be dismissed at the first request of the people; from the privileged body enjoying "sinecures" with high salaries, bourgeois, they become the workers of a "special weapon" whose salaries do not exceed the usual salary of a good worker. Here and there alone is the essence of the Paris Commune as a particular type of State.

Lenin places great emphasis on the participation of the working population in the administration of the State (XXIX, 109):

Work in this field [the fight against bureaucracy], is closely connected with the implementation of the chief historical purpose of Soviet power, i.e., to advance towards the final abolition of the state, and should consist of the following. First, every member of a Soviet must, without fail, do a certain job of state administration; secondly, these jobs must be consistently changed so that they embrace all aspects of government, all its branches; and, thirdly, literally all the working population must be drawn into independent participation in state administration by means of a series of gradual measures that are carefully selected and unfailingly implemented.

And we repeat with Marx, Engels (1872 Preface to the *Communist Manifesto*; XXV, 437) that "The Commune is the first attempt by a proletarian revolution to smash the bourgeois state machine; and it is the political form 'at last discovered', by which the smashed state machine can and must be replaced".

b. 1871, a milestone marking the separation between progressive bourgeois and imperialist wars

In a *Filo del Tempo* entitled "Imperialist War and Revolutionary War" (*Battaglia Comunista* 11, 1950), our party wrote in the line of Lenin: "There are two types of wars. The progressive bourgeois wars, of anti-feudal development, of national liberation; the imperialist wars. The date between the two eras is 1871, the Paris Commune. The movement of the world proletariat gets on the level of the Revolution, it breaks with the Nation".

Or again, the party text *Russia and Revolution in Marxist Theory*, exposed during the general meeting of 31 October–1 November 1954 in Bologna, published in numbers 21–23 of 1954 and 1–8 of 1955 of our press organ in Italian at that time, *Il Programma Comunista*, explains the question as follows: "The European continental area, where the problem of the liberal national revolutions to which the proletariat will give its support during a period ending in 1871 arises. France appears in this area although during the periods 1789–1815 and 1848–1852, it was governed by the bourgeoisie and the Republic was established there".

Since 1871, there has been no more truce between the proletariat and the bourgeoisie

1871 marked the end of all union between the proletariat and the bourgeoisie which, in France during the Paris Commune, preferred to ally itself with the enemy and thus against the interest of the nation it represented in order to fight its proletariat, conscious that the latter was aiming at its destruction as a monopolizing class.

Marx, in an exposé on the Paris Commune of 23 May 1871 at the General Council (M-E, XXII, 595–596), speaks of this connivance between the national bourgeoisies against the Parisian proletariat:

> The Paris Commune was crushed with the help of the Prussians, who assumed the role of gendarmes of Thiers. Bismarck, Thiers, Favre conspired to liquidate the Commune. In Frankfurt, Bismarck acknowledged that Thiers and Favre asked him to intervene. The result shows that he is willing to do everything in his power to help them—without risking the lives of German soldiers, not because he spares human lives when the prospect of loot opens up to him, but because he wants to humiliate the French who are fighting among themselves to be able to extort even more from them. Bismarck allowed Thiers to use more soldiers than the agreement allowed, but he only allowed a limited supply of food to Paris.

And Marx goes on to point out that this is an ancient practice:

All this is nothing but the repetition of ancient practices. The upper classes have always been in agreement when it came to suppressing the working class. In the 11th century, during a war between the French knights and the Normans, the peasants rose up and organized an insurrection. Immediately, the knights forgot their differences and allied themselves to crush the peasant movement. To show how the Prussians acted as policemen, we need only recall that in the city of Rouen they had 500 men arrested on the pretext that they belonged to the International.

The bourgeoisie thus demonstrates with the Commune that it is no longer capable of waging a national war and that its revolutionary role, which began in 1789, clearly ends in 1871. As Lenin tells us, *the democratic bourgeois revolution in France, begun in 1789, ended in 1871*; by affirming this, we place ourselves at the level of the objective historical task of the bourgeois revolution, and by "completion of the democratic bourgeois revolution", we speak of the disappearance of the very substratum capable of giving birth to a bourgeois revolution, of the completion of the complete cycle of bourgeois revolutions.

In *The Civil War...* (M-E, XXII, 353–354), Marx exclaims:

> That, after the most tremendous war of modern times, the conquering and the conquered hosts should fraternize for the common massacre of the proletariat—this unparalleled event does indicate, not, as Bismarck thinks, the final repression of a new society up heaving, but the crumbling into dust of bourgeois society. The highest heroic effort of which old society is still capable is national war; and this is now proved to be a mere governmental humbug, intended to defer the struggle of classes, and to be thrown aside as soon as that class struggle bursts out into civil war. Class rule is no longer able to disguise itself in a national uniform; the national governments are one as against the proletariat! After Whit-Sunday, 1871, there can be neither peace nor truce possible between the working men of France and the appropriators of their produce... But the battle must break out again and again in ever-growing dimensions, and there can be no doubt as to who will be the victor in the end... And the French working class is only the advanced guard of the modern proletariat.

The proletariat as the only revolutionary class

Marx, in *The Civil War...* (M-E, XXII, 336–337), explains:

> It was the first revolution in which the working class was open-
> ly recognized as the only one still capable of social initiative,
> even by the great mass of the middle class of Paris—shopkeep-
> ers, traders, merchants—the rich capitalists excepted. The
> Commune had saved it, by wisely settling this perpetual cause
> of disputes within the middle class itself: the question of credi-
> tors and debtors. This same part of the middle class had partic-
> ipated in the crushing of the workers' insurrection in June
> 1848... In fact, after the exodus from Paris of the entire upper
> Bohemian Bonapartist and capitalist class, the real party of the
> middle-class order showed itself in the form of the "Union
> Républicaine" which enlisted under the colors of the Com-
> mune and defended it against the premeditated falsifications of
> Thiers.

Or again in the first draft of *The Civil War...* (M-E, XXII, 496):

> For the first time in history, the small and middle bourgeoisie
> openly rallied to the workers' revolution and proclaimed that it
> was the only instrument of its own salvation and that of
> France! It constitutes alongside the workers the mass of the
> National Guard, it sits alongside them in the Commune and its
> Republican Union plays a mediating role in their favor... *They*
> *feel that only the working class can emancipate them.*

In fact, with the Dufaure laws, "what the perils of the siege had not been able to
do, the Assembly did: the union of the petty-bourgeoisie with the proletariat"
(Lissagaray), but let's not forget that the only class really determined to fight,
revolutionary in its essence, is the working class which, at the moment of the
carnage, found itself abandoned by its allies of yesterday:

> Only the workers remained loyal to the Commune to the end.
> The bourgeois republicans and the petty bourgeoisie soon
> broke away from it: the former were frightened off by the revo-
> lutionary-socialist, proletarian character of the movement; the
> latter broke away when they saw that it was doomed to in-

evitable defeat.... Deserted by its former allies and left without support, the Commune was doomed to defeat (Lenin, XVII, 140).

The proletariat must organize itself independently of the other classes

"Deep changes have occurred since the great Revolution, class antagonisms have worsened...today, on the other hand, the proletariat can no longer confuse its interests with those of other classes, classes which are hostile to it. Let the bourgeoisie bear the responsibility for the national humiliation! The business of the proletariat is to fight to free labor from the yoke of the bourgeoisie through socialism" (Lenin, XII, 499).

8. WHY THE COMMUNE WAS A FAILURE

"The more we cherish, for instance, the memory of the Paris Commune of 1871, the less permissible is it to refer to it offhand, without analysing its mistakes and the special conditions attending it. To do so would mean repeating the absurd example of the Blanquists—whom Engels ridiculed—who (in 1874, in their "Manifesto") paid homage to every act of the Commune" (Lenin, IX, 80).

"We should imitate not the mistakes it made... but its successful practical measures, which indicate the correct road" (Lenin, IX, 141).

And we can conclude with Lenin that because of these errors, the Commune "was a government as it should not be ours"!

Thus Lenin and Trotsky knew perfectly well the history of the Paris Commune, on whose shoulders the Russian Revolution of 1905 was to be built. But in order to make this new revolutionary leap, they had to develop a serious critique of the errors of the Commune; it is therefore with their help and that of Marx and Engels that we will try to define the weak points of the Commune.

a. Weaknesses and errors

Absence of a single proletarian theory

Let's use Engels' 1891 introduction to *The Civil War...* (M-E, XXVII, 187), to review the political tendencies within the Commune:

> The members of the Commune were divided into a majority of the Blanquists, who had also been predominant in the Central

Committee of the National Guard; and a minority, members of the International Working Men's Association, chiefly consisting of adherents of the Proudhon school of socialism. The great majority of the Blanquists at that time were socialist only by revolutionary and proletarian instinct; only a few had attained greater clarity on the essential principles, through Vaillant, who was familiar with German scientific socialism.... Naturally, the Proudhonists were chiefly responsible for the economic decrees of the Commune, both for their praiseworthy and their un-praiseworthy aspects; as the Blanquists were for its political actions and omissions. And in both cases the irony of history willed—as is usual when doctrinaires come to the helm—that both did the opposite of what the doctrines of their school pre-scribed.

Thus the decisions of the communards were not borrowed from preconceived doctrines, but, as Lenin points out, dictated by the necessity of the facts: the Proudhonians, despite the anti-collectivism and opposition to independent po-litical action by the proletariat of Proudhon, fought in the Labor Commission for the association and federation of workers; and the Blanquists, despite Blan-qui's theory of dictatorial centralization, convinced the French to a free federa-tion of all the communes, to a national organization created by the nation itself, and which overthrew the repressive, centralized force of the government.

As Lenin wrote in *The Two Tactics of Social Democracy* (IX, 80–81), the Com-mune thus had "a workers' government that was unable, and could not at that time, distinguish between the elements of a democratic revolution and a social-ist revolution, a government that confused the tasks of fighting for a republic with those of fighting for socialism".

This absence of proletarian theory, of a precise political program has there-fore resulted in a lack of organization, an abuse of nationalist phrases and eco-nomic and military errors.

Lack of centralized organization

The government of the Commune lacked coherence and cohesion, a fact which can be explained by the diverse political tendencies which coexisted there and by the immaturity of the French workers' movement from the political, eco-nomic and theoretical point of view in the face of a modern revolutionary situa-tion.

The Commune governed in disorder, constantly oscillating between dictatorship and democracy. The heads of the various commissions responsible for ministerial services changed several times, especially in military affairs. It had to dismiss the adventurer Cluseret, who had already questioned Bergeret for the 3 April exit, and by its indecision it discouraged the generous Rossel who preferred to resign.

Dissension within the Commune also concerned the Committee of Public Safety. As the military situation worsened, the 'Jacobins" of the Commune linked to the revolution of 1789 made it difficult to form this committee by 45 votes to 23. The intervention of the latter in the affairs of the war was particularly unfortunate. Renewed with the support of the minority this time, after the resignation of the delegate to the war Rossel, the new Committee of Public Salvation took some sound but too late measures.

While the struggle between the different tendencies, petty-bourgeois and proletarian, and personal rivalries undermined the Commune from within, the continuous interference of the Central Committee of the National Guard in military affairs hindered and sometimes even paralysed its action. The CC had handed over power to the Commune on 26 March and withdrew to the Château d'eau, but it continued to hold meetings and intervene in military affairs. It was it to propose the adventurer Cluseret, at the beginning of April, for the war department. Frequent clashes occurred between the members of the Commune, many of whom were members of this committee, and the CC of the National Guard.

Abuse of revolutionary nationalist phrases and patriotic illusions

Indeed, the French proletariat was not yet free of the "national" illusions that made it fight alongside its bourgeoisie, and prevented it from concentrating its forces for its class organizations.

Lenin, in *The Teachings of the Commune* (XIII, 475)), wrote:

> The patriotic idea had its origin in the Great Revolution of the eighteenth century; it swayed the minds of the socialists of the Commune; and Blanqui, for example, undoubtedly a revolutionary and an ardent supporter of socialism, could find no better title for his newspaper than the bourgeois cry: "The country is in danger!" Combining contradictory tasks—patriotism and socialism—was the *fatal mistake of French socialists*.

Lenin further explains in *Socialism and the War* (XXI, 324):

> Half a century ago, the proletariat was too weak; the objective
> conditions for socialism had not yet matured, there could be no
> coordination and cooperation between the revolutionary
> movements in all the belligerent countries; the "national ideol-
> ogy" (the traditions of 1792), with which a section of the
> Parisian workers were imbued, was a petty-bourgeois weak-
> ness, which Marx noted at the time, and was *one of the causes of
> the downfall of the Commune.*

Marx, in the Second Address of the General Council of London, on 9 September
1870, already warned the French proletariat against a craze for the false national idea, against the tradition of 1792: *the proletariat could no longer confuse its interests with those of other classes.* Let the bourgeoisie bear the responsibility for
the national humiliation! *The business of the proletariat is now to fight for the liberation of labor from the yoke of the bourgeoisie by socialism.* But it was the failure of the
Paris Commune that was to teach this to the French proletariat and to the international labor movement.

Economic errors

Lenin, in *The Teachings of the Commune* (XIII, 476), wrote:

> But two mistakes destroyed the fruits of the splendid victory.
> The proletariat stopped half-way: instead of setting about "ex-
> propriating the expropriators", it allowed itself to be led astray
> by dreams of establishing a higher justice in the country united
> by a common national task; such institutions as the banks, for
> example, were not taken over, and Proudhonist theories about
> a "just exchange", etc., still prevailed among the socialists. The
> second mistake was excessive magnanimity on the part of the
> proletariat: instead of destroying its enemies it sought to exert
> moral influence on them; it underestimated the significance of
> direct military operations in civil war, and instead of launching
> a resolute offensive against Versailles that would have crowned
> its victory in Paris, it tarried and gave the Versailles govern-
> ment time to gather the dark forces and prepare for the blood-
> soaked week of May.

As far as the strictly economic errors were concerned, it was therefore the Proudhonians of the International who took care of the economic part, which explains why "many things were neglected" (M-E, XXVII, 187).

They didn't take the Banque de France!

> "The hardest thing to understand is certainly the holy awe with which they remained standing respectfully outside the gates of the Bank of France. This was also a serious political mistake. The bank in the hands of the Commune—this would have been worth more than 10,000 hostages. It would have meant the pressure of the whole of the French bourgeoisie on the Versailles government in favor of peace with the Commune" (M-E, XXVII, 187).

Lissagaray comments:

> The Commune, in its blind indignation, could not see the real hostages who were gouging out their eyes: the Bank, the Registration and Domains, the Caisse des Dépôts et Consignations, etc.... From there, the testicles of Versailles were held; one could laugh at its experience, its cannons. Without exposing a man, the Commune only had to tell him: "Transact or die". The elected representatives of 26 March were not to dare…

> Since 19 March, the Bank's regents had been waiting every morning for their cash to be executed… From the first meeting with the delegates at the Town Hall, the governor perceived their shyness, battling, seemed to think, spinning his money écu by écu… The Commune had nearly 3 billion on hand, of which almost a billion was in cash, enough to buy a thousand times the Gallifet and high officials of Versailles; for hostages, the 90,000 securities deposits and the two billion in circulation whose deposit was in rue de la Vrillière.

It was the Breton engineer, Charles Victor Beslay, an industrialist and banker who participated in the creation of the Internationale in Paris and who left it before 1871, who was chosen to be the intermediary with the Banque de France. His nonsense of "The Banque de France is the fortune of the country; without it, there is no industry, no trade; if you violate it, all the notes go bankrupt" was well received by the Proudhonians of the Commune. Lissagaray commented: "The capitalist fortress in Versailles did not have any stronger defenders!".

He concluded:

> From the first week, the Commune appeared weak towards the authors of the exit, the CC, the Bank; weak in its decrees, in the choice of its delegate to the War, without a military plan, discussing all the time, the irreconcilable people who remained after the flight of the liberals understood where we were going. Not wanting martyrdom, they resigned.

Democratic illusions and military weakness

"It is still necessary to suppress the bourgeoisie and crush their resistance. This was particularly necessary for the Commune; and one of the reasons for its defeat was that it did not do this with sufficient determination" (Lenin, XXV, p.424).

In fact, neither the CC and even less the Commune, where universal suffrage had brought in more bourgeois elements, wanted civil war; they did not therefore devote much attention to strategy (the 3 April exit was a catastrophic failure), nor to the organization of the communal army, the National Guard.

The excessive magnanimity of the Communards made the Commune exercise an equally "magnanimous" proletarian dictatorship. It was well aware of its weakness and tried to strengthen itself through the creation of the Committee of Public Safety; it was a lost cause; too few communards were convinced of the *necessity of using violence against the bourgeoisie*, which, however, spared no means to fight the insurgents.

Trotsky, in 1921, in *Lessons of the Paris Commune*, specifies that all the ministers should have been taken prisoner with Thiers in mind; that a few dozen or a few hundred devoted workers should have been incorporated into the retreating armies with the aim of arousing the discontent of the soldiers against the officers and then bringing them back to Paris. No one thought of this.

There were many military faults. Marx wrote to Kugelman on April 12, 1871 (M-E, XLIV, 132):

> If they are defeated only their "decency" will be to blame. They should have marched at once on Versailles, after first Vinoy and then the reactionary section of the Paris National Guard had themselves retreated. The right moment was missed because of conscientious scruples. They did not want to start the

> civil war... Second mistake: The Central Committee surrendered its power too soon, to make way for the Commune. Again from a too "honourable" scrupulousness!

Indeed, the CC had shown irresolution by not marching from 19 March on Versailles, then defenseless, and by not occupying strategic forts such as Mont Valérien. Moreover, it gave up power too soon to the Commune, because the military problem was much more urgent than the legal one, and thinking of holding Commune elections on 26 March (as on 16 April) and tedious talks with the mayors of Paris meant wasting precious time.

Democratic and autonomist illusions were equally negative. With the elections and the talks, the CC was seeking to clear its responsibility. Still in the same text, Trotsky wrote that the CC only sought to replace the developing proletarian revolution with petty-bourgeois reform: communal autonomy, whereas the real revolutionary task consisted in assuring the proletariat of power throughout the country. To reach this goal, it was necessary to defeat Versailles without wasting time, sending agitators and organizers of the armed force throughout France. Instead of this offensive policy of aggression, which alone could save the situation, the rulers of Paris locked themselves up in an idealistic chatter about communal autonomy (each city has the sacred right of self-government!) to mask their cowardice in the face of revolutionary action. And Trotsky concludes the question—thinking of the PCF—in 1921: "

> The hostility to centralist organization—a heritage of petty bourgeois localism and autonomism—is without a doubt the weak side of a certain section of the French proletariat.... The tendency towards particularism, whatever the form it may assume, is a heritage of the dead past.

Fear of civil war also reigned. The Commune neglected military strategy, not for lack of men who were up to the task – Generals Dombrowsky and Wroblevsky, men full of ardour like Duval and Flourens, etc. – but for lack of conviction, political awareness, fear of illegality and above all fear of civil war.

Marx wrote to Wilhelm Liebknecht on 6 April 1871 (M-E, XLIV, 128):

> It seems the Parisians are succumbing. It is their own fault but a fault which really was due to their too great honnêté. The Central Committee and later the Commune gave that MISCHIEVOUS avorton, Thiers, time to consolidate hostile forces,

in the first place by their folly of not wanting to start a civil war —as if Thiers had not already started it by his attempt at forcibly disarming Paris, as if the National Assembly, summoned merely to decide the question of war or peace with the Prussians, had not immediately declared war on the Republic! Secondly, in order that the appearance of having usurped power should not attach to them, they lost precious moments (they should immediately have advanced on Versailles after the defeat (Place Vendôme) of the réactionnaires in Paris).

The National Guard was not a Red Army. Trotsky, the military strategist of the Russian Revolution, clearly showed the defects of this "Red Army" in the text *The Teachings of the Commune:*

> The Central Committee of the National Guard is in effect a Council of Deputies of the armed workers and the petty bourgeoisie. Such a Council, elected directly by the masses who have taken the revolutionary road, represents an excellent apparatus of action. But at the same time, and just because of its immediate and elementary connection with the masses who are in the state in which the revolutionary has found them, it reflects not only all the strong sides but also the weak sides of the masses, and it reflects at first the weak sides still more than it does the strong: it manifests the spirit of indecision, of waiting, the tendency to be inactive after the first successes. The Central Committee of the National Guard needed to be led.

The army of the Commune, the National Guard, thus suffered from a lack of cohesion. The National Guards were revolutionary fighters who were repugnant to an indispensable discipline. Trotsky explains that the eligibility of the leaders and the ease with which they could be dismissed was a source of weakness rather than strength.

> Varlin formulated the claim that the entire command of the National Guard from top to bottom should be elected by the National Guards themselves.

> Electability, democratic methods, are but one of the instruments in the hands of the proletariat and its party. Electability

can in no wise be a fetish, a remedy for all evils. The methods of electability must be combined with those of appointments. The power of the Commune came from the elected National Guard. But once created, the Commune should have reorganized with a strong hand the National Guard, from top to bottom, given it reliable leaders and established a régime of very strict discipline. The Commune did not do this, being itself deprived of a powerful revolutionary directing center. So it was crushed.

However, the issue must be seen from a political and military point of view. On the political side, this measure made it possible to purge the National Guard of the counter-revolutionary command and to split the army into two parts along class lines. But on the military side, the liberation of the army from the old command apparatus inevitably led to the weakening of the cohesion of the organization and the lowering of the combative force. The elected command is most often rather weak on the technical-military side and in terms of maintaining order and discipline. It is therefore necessary to give a revolutionary command, and this cannot be ensured by simple elections, because soldiers cannot be expected to acquire the experience of choosing their command well. Therefore, selection measures from above must be used, and this is the role of the party. Trotsky concludes: "If particularism and democratic autonomism are extremely dangerous to the proletarian revolution in general, they are ten times more dangerous to the army. We saw that in the tragic example of the Commune".

It is also in his work *Terrorism and Communism* (1920) that Trotsky mentions the Commune's army. Thus, despite the magnificent warlike qualities of the Parisian workers, indecision and the spirit of conciliation at the top had led to disintegration at the base. While 162,000 simple soldiers and 6,500 officers were paid, the number who actually went into battle varied between 20,000 and 30,000. As a result, the federations lacked a precise and centralized leadership apparatus.

The carelessness of the military apparatus (poor material organization, inconsistency of orders) quickly killed discipline. "The brave men only wanted to be relieved by themselves, the others dodged the service; the officers did the same" comments Lissagaray.

Competition between the CC and the Commune was another weakness. The CC hastened to hand over its powers to the representatives of the Commune, which needed a broader democratic basis, as Trotsky always tells us. It was already a big mistake to play elections at that time, but once the elections were held and the Commune was united, everything had to be concentrated in the Commune. The CC remained a political force competing with the Commune, which deprived the latter of energy and the necessary firmness in military matters.

> The conduct of the war was not the strong side of the Commune. That is why it was crushed—and how mercilessly crushed!... The Russian workers have shown that they are capable of mastering the "war machine" as well. Here we see a gigantic step forward in relation to the Commune.... We are taking one blow at a time to our executioners. *We are taking vengeance for the Commune, and we shall avenge it* (in *Terrorism and Communism*, New Park Publications, p. 105).

b. Immaturity of the Communist Party

The "revolutionary spontaneity" of the proletariat cannot suffice to win the victory over the centralized, ruthless and economically powerful bourgeoisie. The armed insurrection and the military conduct of the civil war cannot be left to the chance of the mobilization of the masses. The fact that, as Trotsky points out, under qualitatively similar conditions the Bolsheviks of 1917 achieved what the communards of 1871 missed, highlights the primordial role of a structured and firm revolutionary party. Already Marx, in the second address of the International, advised the Parisian workers to organize themselves by taking advantage of the freedom brought by the Republic. Above all, we must not exalt with Kautsky the glory of the "spontaneism" of the Communards, which in fact constituted their weakness.

As we have already seen above, there was no fully developed proletarian theory in the French workers' movement of the time, and this precisely because there was not yet a completely autonomous party, a class party as Marx and Engels meant it. Thus in a letter to G. Trier of 18 December 1889 (M-E, XLVIII, 423), Engels affirms: " *If the proletariat is to be strong enough to win on the crucial day, it is essential—and Marx and I have been advocating this ever since 1847—for it to constitute a party in its own right, distinct from and opposed to all the rest, one that is conscious of itself as a class party*".

But in the nineteenth century, capitalism in France was not very developed. Its proletariat was therefore weak, badly organized, as Lenin explains in *In Memory of the Commune* (XVII, 141):

> French capitalism was still poorly developed, and France was at that time mainly a petty-bourgeois country (artisans, peasants, shopkeepers, etc.). On the other hand, there was no workers' party; the working class had not gone through a long school of struggle and was unprepared, and for the most part did not even clearly visualise its tasks and the methods of fulfilling them. There was no serious political organisation of the proletariat, nor were there strong trade unions and co-operative societies...

The French Marxist party will be born after the French socialists' access to scientific socialism. In the Commune, only Frankel was initiated into Marx's theories, and Vaillant during his London exile would spread them in Blanquist circles.

It is Trotsky again who tells us in the already quoted text on the Paris Commune how the action of a Marxist party would have been decisive.

Comparing the revolutionary movement of 1871 with that of November 1917, Trotsky shows us admirably how the Paris Commune suffered from the absence of a truly Marxist party. He defines the "workers' party" as follows:

> The workers' party—the real one, is not a machine for parliamentary manoeuvres, it is the accumulated and organized experience of the proletariat. It is only with the aid of the party, which rests upon the whole history of its past, which foresees theoretically the paths of development, all its stages, and which extracts from it the necessary formula of action, that the proletariat frees itself from the need of always recommencing its history: its hesitations, its lack of decision, its mistakes. The proletariat of Paris did not have such a party.

Trotsky then specifies methodically how the action of a workers' party would have radically changed the course of events. *First of all, the Commune came too late.* It had every possibility of taking power on September 4, which would have allowed the proletariat of Paris to put itself at the head of the workers in their struggle against the forces of the past, against Bismarck and against Thiers. The masses were groping around, and the absence of a party had as a result that *the revolution broke out six months too late* while Paris was surrounded: six months passed before the proletariat had re-established in its memory the lessons of the past revolutions, and seized power. "These six months proved to be an irreparable loss. If the centralized party of revolutionary action had been found at the head of the proletariat of France in September 1870, the whole history of France, and with it the whole history of humanity, would have taken another direction."

Indeed, the role of the party is to choose the most favorable moment for the revolution and obviously in connection with the masses: *it intervenes consciously*. But if the proletariat of Paris seized power, it did not do so consciously but because its enemies took the initiative to challenge it by abandoning it. *"The revolution fell upon it unexpectedly."*

Marx, first draft to *The Civil War...* (M-E, XXII, 481) writes:

> The victorious establishment at Paris of the Commune in the beginning of November 1870... would not only have taken the defence out of the hands of traitors and imprinted its enthusiasm as the present heroic war of Paris shows, it would have altogether changed the character of the war. It would have become the war of republican France, hoisting the flag of the social Revolution of the nineteenth century, against Prussia, the banner bearer of the conquest and counterrevolution".

With the party at the head of the revolution, the proletarian dictatorship would have been more severe:

> In the midst of great events, moreover, such decisions can be adopted only by a revolutionary party which looks forward to a revolution, prepares for it, does not lose its head, by a party which is accustomed to having a rounded view and is not afraid to act (Trotsky, *Lessons of the Paris Commune*).

We have already seen above how a Marxist party would have done better to turn the National Guard into a Red Army. Trotsky adds:

> A strong party leadership is needed. More than any other proletariat has the French made sacrifices for the revolution. But also more than any other has it been duped...Those fighters of

'71 were not lacking in heroism. What they lacked was clarity in method and a centralized leading organization. That is why they were vanquished.

But let us not forget that this text was written in 1921, when the PCF was already experiencing its first dramas and its first deficiencies. By insisting on the need for a party depositary of the experience of the international proletariat, centralized and clear in theory, he warns the PCF.

It is obvious that we cannot simply conclude that the failure of the Commune is directly due to the absence of a communist party leading the movement, but with Marx, Engels, Lenin we affirm that the social situation of France in 1871 was not ripe for revolutionary success, nor consequently for the formation of a proletarian party conscious of its revolutionary task. France could not produce this at that time. *The Commune of 1871 was the forerunner of the world proletarian revolution,* but it was an *"assault on heaven";* and the Russian Revolution of 1917 was helped by the experience of the Commune, its contributions and its errors, and was born of material conditions more favorable to the explosion of a revolutionary communist movement and thus to the development of a Communist Party.

Indeed, the conditions in France were not ripe for a proletarian revolution; and Marx, who foresaw the insurrection of 1871, was therefore hardly favorable to it. Lenin (*The Teachings of the Commune,* XIII, 476) concludes: "But despite all its mistakes the Commune was a superb example of the great proletarian movement of the nineteenth century".

CONCLUSION

The historical significance of the Commune

Let Lenin speak once again:

> Marx, however, was not only enthusiastic about the heroism of the Communards, who, as he expressed it, "stormed heaven". Although the mass revolutionary movement did not achieve its aim, he regarded it as a historic experience of enormous importance, as a certain advance of the world proletarian revolution, as a practical step that was more important than hundreds of programmes and arguments. Marx endeavored to analyze this experiment, to draw tactical lessons from it and re-examine his theory in the light of it. (XXV, p.418–419).

And Lenin reminds us once again what this *step forward*, this "new starting point of world historical importance" (as Marx wrote to Kugelmann on 17 April 1871), consists of:

> Marx set a high value on the historic significance of the Commune—if, during the treacherous attempt by the Versailles gang to seize the arms of the Paris proletariat, the workers had allowed themselves to be disarmed without a fight, the disastrous effect of the demoralization, that this weakness would have caused in the proletarian movement, would have been far, far greater than the losses suffered by the working class in the battle to defend its arms. The sacrifices of the Commune, heavy as they were, are made up for by their significance for the general struggle of the proletariat: it stirred the socialist movement throughout Europe, it demonstrated the strength of civil war, it dispelled patriotic illusions, and destroyed the naïve belief in any efforts of the bourgeoisie for common national aims. The Commune taught the European proletariat to pose concretely the tasks of the socialist revolution" (XIII, p.476–77).

The impulse given to the international proletarian movement

The massacres of the Commune and the international repression of the IWMA disoriented the workers' movement for a moment, but for a short time. A few years after the crushing of the Commune, the French workers' movement was reborn:

> The bourgeoisie were satisfied. "Now we have finished with socialism for a long time," said their leader, the blood thirsty dwarf, Thiers… Less than six years after the suppression of the Commune, when many of its champions were still pining in prison or in exile, a new working-class movement arose in France… And in another few years, the new workers' party and the agitational work launched by it throughout the country compelled the ruling classes to release Communards who were still kept in prison by the government (Lenin, XVII, 142–143).

The Commune also allowed the sudden start of the nascent German workers' movement which took over and was based on the Marxist theory of the proletariat, itself the synthesis of the European workers' movements. Engels wrote in 1874 (Preface to *The Peasants' War*), a text quoted by Lenin (V, 371–372):

> The German workers have two important advantages over those of the rest of Europe. First, they belong to the most theoretical people of Europe… "The second advantage is that, chronologically speaking, the Germans were about the last to come into the workers' movement. Just as German theoretical socialism will never forget that it rests on the shoulders of Saint-Simon, Fourier, and Owen—three men who, in spite of all their fantastic notions and all their utopianism, have their place among the most eminent thinkers of all times, and whose genius anticipated innumerable things, the correctness of which is now being scientifically proved by us—so the practical workers' movement in Germany ought never to forget that it has developed on the shoulders of the English and French movements, that it was able simply to utilise their dearly bought experience, and could now avoid their mistakes, which in their time were mostly unavoidable. Without the precedent of the English trade unions and French workers' political struggles, without the gigantic impulse given especially by the Paris Commune, where would we be now?".

In fact, with the Commune, the French workers' movement passed the torch to the German one, thus allowing the affirmation of the preponderance of Marxist theory over that of Proudhon. On July 20, 1870, Marx wrote to Engels: "The preponderance of the German working class over the French in world theatre would at the same time mean the preponderance of our theory over that of Proudhon".

In his introduction to *The Civil War...* in 1891, Engels added that "...the Commune was also the grave of the Proudhon school of socialism".

Finally, the magnificent Russian revolution did not forget the lessons of the Paris Commune, and considered itself as its direct heir. Lenin repeats it many times:

> The lesson learnt by the proletariat will not be forgotten. The working class will make use of it, as it has already done in Russia during the December uprising (XIII, 477).

> We shall see further on that the Russian revolutions of 1905 and 1917, in different circumstances and under different conditions, continue the work of the Commune and confirm Marx's brilliant historical analysis (Lenin, XXV, 437).

> We are in a different situation because, having climbed on the shoulders of the Paris Commune and taking advantage of the long development of German social democracy, we can see clearly what we are doing by creating the power of the Soviets.

And if the Bolsheviks claimed to be part of the Paris Commune, we refer today to the Russian proletarian State which is our model for tomorrow, and throw in the face of the bourgeoisie these words of Marx (exposed at the General Council of 23 May 1871(M-E, XXII, 595): *"But if the Commune is defeated, the fight is simply deferred. The principles of the Commune are eternal and cannot be crushed: they will assert themselves again until the working classes are emancipated".*